1001 Things To Do FREE In Arizona

Jim Morse

PHOENIX BOOKS/PUBLISHERS
P.O. Box 32008
Phoenix, Arizona 85064
USA

ACKNOWLEDGEMENTS

I am indebted to Margaret Harris and her daughters Christina and Lisa for their encouragement and research assistance; to Pete Tufts, a friend and writer from Tucson who helped with the chapters on ghost towns and historic sites; and also to the Arizona Office of Tourism and chambers of commerce throughout the state for their contributions. — JM

Published by Phoenix Books/Publishers, P.O. Box 32008, Phoenix, Arizona USA.

Printed in the United States of America.

ISBN: 0-914778-39-0

NOTE FROM THE AUTHOR

This book was written to serve as a general guide to the more important places and events in Arizona that are free for the viewing or doing, where visitors may play, explore, photograph and otherwise enjoy to their hearts' content. The material in each chapter is divided by geographic areas to make it easier for users to plan trips from wherever they happen to be. Sources for additional information are provided in the back of the book.

PUBLISHER'S NOTE: Some sites or events may have instituted admission charges since the publication of this book. Also, a few places where admission is free do accept donations that are strictly voluntary.

Portions of this book are adapted from *Insiders' Guide: Phoenix-Scottsdale-Tempe-Mesa-Tucson* and *Outdoor Recreation in Arizona* with permission of the publisher.

TABLE OF CONTENTS

Arizona in Profile

Arizona is a land of striking contrasts — a fact clear even to the most nonchalant and unobservant traveler who has had the experience of passing through the state's high mountain country, canyons, expansive deserts and scenic valley's and catching a glimpse of its many lakes, rivers and mountain streams.

Long before Julius Caesar ruled the Roman Empire, numerous Indian tribes had flourishing civilizations going in this varied and rich land. High, almost inaccessible multi-storied cliff dwellings today stand in silent tribute to some of these prehistoric cultures. The Ho-Ho-Kams, who lived in the Valley of the Sun but mysteriously vanished before Columbus visited the New World, laid down a system of irrigation canals whose patterns are followed to this day.

The year 1539 marks the beginning of Arizona's written history. It was in that year that Spaniards sent exploration parties northward from what is now Mexico. In 1821, when Mexico declared her independence from Spain, the Mexican flag flew over what was to become the Arizona Territory. When the American war with Mexico ended in 1848, everything north of the Gila River went to the United States.

The Gadsden Purchase in 1853 accounted for the rest of what is now Arizona. For a brief period, in 1861, the flag of the Confederacy flew over the southern part of the state, and a Civil War battle of sorts was fought at Picacho Pass north of Tucson.

With the conclusion of the Civil War, America's great westward migration began and pioneers from "back East" began settling in Arizona, particularly after rich gold and silver deposits were discovered. By 1866 the territory was opened for the miner, farmer and rancher - a situation which led, of course, to the protracted series of battles which came to be known as the Indian Wars. The bitter clashes between native tribes and invading cavalry ended with the surrender of Geronimo in 1886.

These decades of Arizona's history have, of course, provided movie-makers and authors with a wealth of exciting and adventure-packed frontier drama. In 1912, with her lawless, rugged days rapidly giving way to a more ordered 20th Century, Arizona became the nation's 48th state.

Although man has lived in the area for more than 20,000 years, native-born Arizonans are still outnumbered by newcomers from other states. A blending of modern home construction and industry, a frontier heritage of vigor and romance, and a future promising steady economic and cultural growth, continues each year to attract thousands of families who have been encouraged by the "Go West" bug to settle in this intriguing place of high mountains and hot deserts.

HISTORICAL HIGHLIGHTS

20,000 BC—First evidence of prehistoric man's existence in this part of the Southwest.

800 AD—Indians lived in caves along Rio Puerco and in numerous other areas.

1100—Pottery-making cliff-dwellers lived in Walnut Canyon.

1200—Oraibi, the oldest known community in the United States, came into being (and is still thriving today).

1300—Indian farmers in the Gila and Salt River valleys built and used irrigation canals totaling 185 miles.

1539—Franciscan Friar Marcos de Niza searched for the Seven Cities of Cibola. He is the first white man definitely known to have explored Arizona.

1692-1701—Padre Kino and other Jesuits built missions in southern Arizona, including the beautiful San Xavier del Bac, 9 miles south of Tucson.

1751—Pima and Papago uprising forced abandonment of all Spanish missions.

1767—The Jesuits were ordered to leave New Spain (which included what is now Mexico and Arizona).

1824—The Republic of Mexico was founded and the Territoria de Nuevo Mexico, which included the present day states of Arizona and New Mexico, was formed.

1827—Arizona's "mission" era ended when Mexico expelled the Franciscans.

1846—The United States declared war on Mexico.

1848—The Mexican War ended with Mexico giving up all claims north of the Gila River.

1850—Congress made Arizona part of New Mexico territory

1853—The Gadsden Purchase was negotiated for $10 million, giving the United States all land south of the Gila River to the present-day Mexican-U.S. border.

1861—Settlers in southern Arizona organized the Confederate Territory of Arizona.

1862—A brief Civil War skirmish at Picacho Pass returned loose control over the area to the Union.

1863—Congress created the Territory of Arizona.

1864—Fort Whipple became the first site for the territorial government which subsequently moved to Prescott, then to Tucson, back to Prescott, and finally to Phoenix in 1889.

1877-83—Two railroad lines traversed the state from east and west.

1880—The city of Phoenix was incorporated.

1886—Geronimo was captured, marking the end of the American-Indian wars.

1911—Roosevelt Dam, the first in a series of dams on Salt River, was dedicated.

1912—Arizona became the 48th state on February 14th.

******

MOTTO: Ditat Deus (God Enriches)
FLOWER: Saguaro Blossom
BIRD: Cactus Wren
LENGTH: 390 miles
BREADTH: 355 miles
ELEVATION: From 137 ft. (Colorado River at Yuma) to 12,655 ft. (San Francisco Peaks)
TREE: Palo Verde

IMPORTANT PHONE NUMBERS

Phoenix Area

Arizona Automobile Association.................. 252-7751
Arizona Highway Patrol 262-8011
Arizona Office of Tourism....................... 255-3618
Phoenix & Valley of the Sun Convention &
Visitors Bureau 957-0070
National Weather Service........................ 261-4000
Department of Fish & Game 942-3000
Arizona State Parks 255-4174
Phoenix Bus Route Information 257-8426
Phoenix Civic Plaza, Box Office 262-7272
Information on Flooding 262-6443
If You Need A Policeman 262-6151
Phoenix Public Library, Main Branch 262-6451
Phoenix Sky Harbor International Airport 273-3377
Phoenix Metropolitan Chamber of Commerce 254-5521
Phoenix Parks and Recreation Department 262-6711
Time and Temperature............................ 258-7600
Recreation Division, Maricopa County
(Parks and Lakes)............................... 262-3711

Scottsdale

Scottsdale Chamber of Commerce 945-8481
Scottsdale Department of Parks 994-2436
Scottsdale Memorial Hospital 994-9616
Scottsdale Police Department 946-6511
Scottsdale Public Library....................... 994-2471

Tempe

Tempe Chamber of Commerce 967-7891
Tempe Community Hospital 968-9411
Tempe Department of Parks 968-8381
Tempe Post Office 894-2128

Mesa

Mesa Chamber of Commerce	969-1307
Mesa Department of Parks	834-2351
Mesa Lutheran Hospital	834-1211
Mesa General Hospital	969-9111
Mesa Post Office	969-9171

Tucson

AAA Automobile Club	296-7461
Chamber of Commerce of Tucson	792-1212
Community Center	791-4266
Game & Fish Department	882-5376
Highway Patrol	883-5376
Police Department	791-4411
Poison Control Centers	
St. Joseph's Hospital	296-3211
St. Mary's Hospital	622-5833
Tucson General Hospital	327-5431
Tucson Medical Center	327-5461
Sheriff's Office	622-3366
Tucson Parks & Recreation Department	791-4873

CHAPTER I

SCENIC WONDERS

Perhaps nowhere in America is there as much variety of scenery as in Arizona. Whether it is the seemingly endless forests of the Mogollon Rim, the snow-peaked San Francisco Mountains in winter or the fragrant colors of desert flowers at springtime, Arizona offers its highways and byways free of tolls and fees of any kind.

There are lakes and mountains, the fabulous Grand Canyon, and a variety of other natural wonders such as the Petrified Forest and The Painted Desert.

We have listed some of the most spectacular samples of this wonderworld of nature. However, if you plan a trip to any area mentioned, the ride will be an unforgettable one. In preparing for any car journey in Arizona, take plenty of extra color film, and test your camera equipment before leaving. Do not miss any opportunity to capture this breathtaking land in slides or prints.

CENTRAL & NORTHERN ARIZONA

(Within a 125 mile radius of Phoenix and Scottsdale)

Cave Creek-Carefree

Carefree, Arizona is one of the most beautiful planned communities in America. It is truly a joy for sightseers, surrounded by desert foothills and unusual rock formations. Carefree is only about an hour's drive from central Phoenix. It can be reached quite easily from Phoenix. Take 7th Street North to Dunlap. At Dunlap turn onto Cave Creek Road and follow it north all the way to Carefree. From Scottsdale, the route is straight out

Scottsdale Road going north until you reach Carefree. If you take Cave Creek Road from North Phoenix, stop as you approach Carefree to examine markers the state has placed to identify the many splendid cacti.

Superstition Mountains

These are the most famous of Arizona's mountains, steeped in legends of lost gold. They lie massive and ominous-looking on the east side of the Valley of the Sun, with a good entry point at Apache Junction, near Mesa.

To reach from the Phoenix-Scottsdale area, go east on U.S. 60 through Mesa. In Mesa Route 60 corresponds to Main Street, which becomes Apache Trail on the outskirts of the city. There are camping areas, hiking and horse trails in the foothills of the Superstitions.

Southwest Aboretum

This veritable wonderland of plants is located between Florence Junction and Superior on US Highway 60. It appears on some maps as the *Boyce Thompson Aborteum,* in honor of its founder. Here one can see every form of beautiful desert plant life from Arizona and around the world. The scenic walking trails and peacefulness about the place makes it a very worthwhile stop.

Oak Creek Canyon

This scenic Arizona spot is near Sedona on the way north to Flagstaff. Take Route 17 north from Phoenix. Your exit marked "Sedona" - Route 89A.

People have called this spot "the second most beautiful canyon in Arizona," next only to the Grand Canyon. It is deep and narrow and has many summer homes and campsites set amid oak and pine trees. One can also spot an occasional apple orchard. It is especially colorful in early November.

Salt River Canyon

Located on U. S. 60 north of Globe. Only the Grand Canyon has more majesty, but because of an excellent highway, the Salt River Canyon can be seen *close up.* After road construction was completed on the four-lane highway through the canyon, Pre-Cambrian rocks were exposed. Geologists estimate that these rocks date back 500 million years.

Sedona-Red Rock Country

Sedona is one of the most popular resort areas in the West. Once there, you are in the center of a vast mountainous wonderland. The area is famous for unique red rock sculptures (Bell Rock, Cathedral Rock, Court House Rock) that tower over the canyon floors in statuesque splendor. An auto trip is a sheer delight.

Sedona is located at the mouth of Oak Creek Canyon. From Phoenix, it is approximately 115 miles via Route 17 (Black Canyon Highway) North. The exit is marked SEDONA, 89A. Drive as slowly as safety will allow and make several stops to photograph all the colorful sights. From Flagstaff, Sedona is a much shorter trip. Take 179 South. The drive takes less than an hour.

The following sights are in a radius of 150-300 miles from Central Arizona.

Grand Canyon*

This is one of the world's greatest natural wonders. For 200 miles the Colorado River flows through this awesome, majestic canyon. From the rim of the canyon a mile above, the river appears like a mere thread. A visit here is a must.

The South Rim of the canyon, which is the one most often visited, is reached via Arizona Highway 64 or US 180 from the Flagstaff area. The remote North Rim of the canyon, open only in summer, is accessible only via Arizona 67 from Jacob's Lake in the Kaibab National Forest.

***There is a parking fee for visitors' cars at the Grand Canyon National Park.**

Painted Desert

This has been called the most beautiful desert in the world. It is visible for 25 miles along US 40, northwest of Holbrook. Mesas and gullies stand out in startling hues, brushstroked by nature. There are several good vantage points on the road for photographs. Sunsets are particularly striking here.

Petrified Forest National Park

This scenic wonder is only 20 miles east of Holbrook. It is literally "an outdoor museum" with petrified logs as large as 100 feet long and six feet in diameter. Thousands of these great logs, some with brilliant jasper and agate colors, lie scattered all about.

There are actually six separate forests in this incredible replica of the past.

Sunset Crater Monument

Here is a 1,000 feet high cone-shaped crater which is moon-like in appearance and yet tremendously colorful. It is grey at the base and tapers to a red tip which reflects the rays of the sun with startling beauty. The turnoff to the crater is located approximately 10 miles north of Flagstaff on Highway 89A.

SOUTHERN ARIZONA

(Within a 25-to-75 mile drive from Tucson)

Cochise Stronghold

This famous place is located 10 miles from US Highway 666, secluded in the Dragoon Mountains. It received its name because the legendary Apache Indian Chief, Cochise, used it as a fortress or stronghold for many years. Today it is a popular camping area.

Mt. Lemmon

This majestic 9,000 feet mountain is in the Santa Catalina chain. It is only a 60-minute drive, east of Tucson. The ride from "Old Pueblo" is scenic and enjoyable. There are magnificient panoramic views on the way to the top. There is also a ski resort at the peak which is open in season. It is the southernmost ski resort in the United States.

Pinal Pioneer Parkway

This is a pleasurable 30-mile stretch of highway on US 80 - 81 from Oracle Junction, near Tucson, northward. It is noted for its scenic beauty and absence of billboards.

Sabino Canyon

A beautiful canyon only 13 miles east of Tucson, extending into the Santa Catalina mountains from the desert floor. It has picturesque streams, horse trails, campgrounds, cottonwood and sycamore trees and cacti.

Saguaro National Monument

This is "Arizona Country," the kind of desert wilderness visitors associate with the state. It is actually divided into two parts, one adjacent to the Rincon Mountain, the other bordering on Old Tucson. One entry point is 17 miles southwest of Tucson.

Both areas cover some 60,000 acres of the finest examples of Saguaro cactus seen anywhere. Giant Saguaros grow to 50 feet high and some are more than 200 years old.

REMOTE AREAS

The Arizona Strip

Here is 750,000 acres of colorful country and a land of spectacular contrasts. Geographically, it is that portion of Arizona north of the Colorado River; a lonely land, but ideal for rockhounds, photographers, off-road vehicles, nature lovers and backpackers. It has green forests, deep canyons and long stretches of open grazing land.

It is rich in history; for here is where hostile Indians gathered, and range wars flared.

Caution: Do not go here without planning, and taking adequate food, water, other supplies and maps. For more information, write: Arizona Strip District Office
196 East Tabernacle
St. George, Utah 84770

SCENIC DRIVES

Thanks to the diverse topography and the many climatic zones caused by sharp changes in elevation, Arizona has literally dozens of outstanding scenic drives. Some sections of both the state and interstate highways are among the most picturesque in the United States. Several of the more interesting and attractive drives in the state are briefly described here:

Ajo

A 21-mile AJO MOUNTAIN SCENIC LOOP and a 51-mile PUERTO BLANCO DRIVE are within the boundaries of Organ Pipe National Monument juist south of Ajo. Highlights include natural history, unusual desert flora, glimpses of wild desert animals and widespread scenic vistas.

Apache Junction

The famous APACHE TRAIL (State Highway 88) is 76 miles long (not counting several short side trips). It loops north and east back to US 60 near Miami and Globe. Highlights include Apache and Roosevelt Lakes, Fish Creek Hill and Canyon, Superstition Mountains Wilderness Area, Tortilla Flat, Roosevelt Dam, recreation areas, former mining sites, Tonto National Monument, and exceptionally fine scenic vistas.

Chinle

The RIM DRIVE is located inside Canyon de Chelly National Monument. Highlights include excellent views of the steepwalled gorge and Indian cliff dwellings such as the "White House."

Douglas

BONITA CANYON DRIVE is within the boundaries of the Chiricahua National Monument. Highlights include odd rock formations, panoramic views of the "Wonderland of Rocks," and nearby ranchlands and mountains.

Flagstaff

SCHULZ PASS ROAD is off US 180 east to US 89. Changing views of the majestic San Francisco Peaks, Elden Mountains, and old volcanic sections now covered with forests and meadows are the major sights along this drive.

Globe

US 60 north of Globe runs through dramatic, mountainous cattle country, the San Carlos and Fort Apache Indian Reservations, and the extremely colorful Salt River Canyon.

Grand Canyon Village

SOUTH RIM DRIVE features eight miles to the west and 25 miles to the east of spectacular views of the world's most famous canyon. Along the North Rim is the 22-mile CAPE ROYAL DRIVE.

Jerome

US 89A through Jerome and winding down to the Verde Valley, offers lovely views of the spreading Valley and Coconino Plateau. A back road to Williams, via Perkinsville, takes in remote cattle country, sections of the Verde Valley, flagstone quarry operations, and side roads to White Horse Lake, Sycamore Canyon and Bill Williams Mountain.

Monument Valley

A self-guided drive from park headquarters shows off some of the many unique formations and breathtaking panoramas of Monument Valley. For those with the time and inclination, horseback exploration of the region is highly recommended. The Visitor Center is four miles southeast of US 163 just south of the Utah border.

Nogales

GHOST TRAIL ALONG THE BORDER is a full day's outing beginning on Highway 82 about five miles north of Nogales and twisting eastward through Washington Camp, Lochiel and Coronado National Memorial to Highway 92 and Bisbee. Highlights include ghost towns, old mines, huge cattle ranches, views of Mexico, canyons and mountains, wide panoramas, lake and recreational sites, nature walks, hiking and numerous historical points.

Payson

MOGOLLON RIM DRIVES are all lovely and scenic during any season. Highways 160 and 87 lead to national forests and to other roads. Highlights: gorgeous forested mountain scenes, lake recreation, forest camping and historic points.

Phoenix

DOBBINS LOOKOUT DRIVE in South Mountain Park (at the extreme south end of Central Avenue) provides an excellent birds-eye view of metropolitan Phoenix. A nighttime drive illustrates why Phoenix is often called a "Jewel in the Desert."

Portal

CAVE CREEK CANYON DRIVE, to the west, shows off rugged, brillaintly-tinted red rhyolite cliffs and other interesting formations. Also highlighted are oak, juniper and pine forests; trout lakes, national forest campgrounds; and the nearby ghost town of Paradise.

Prescott

IRON SPRINGS LOOP, SENATOR HIGHWAY, SKULL VALLEY DRIVE and several primitive roads in the Prescott National offer fine scenery and recreation. Contact the National Forest Service in Phoenix for more detailed maps and other information. The address is 230 N. 1st Avenue, phone 261-3205.

Safford

SWIFT TRAIL is a 36-mile mountain-climbing road from US 666 south of Safford to the 10,700 foot high Mt. Graham. Highlights include wide-ranging vistas, five climatic zones, forest campgrounds and Riggs Flat Lake.

Sedona

SCHNEBLEY HILL, a logging road, leaves Highway 179 at the end of Oak Creek bridge and runs northward. Primary attractions include dramatic close-up views of colorful red-rock formations, beautiful view of Oak Creek Canyon, Sedona, Verde Valley and distant mountains.

US 89A runs northward from Sedona through the heart of lovely Oak Creek Canyon for some 12 miles. Highlights: camp and picnic grounds, lodges, scenic red rock formations, creek fishing and numerous viewpoints.

Springerville

The famed CORONADO TRAIL (US 666) runs south from Springerville for about 90 miles to Clifton, and traverses areas through which the Spanish explorer Francisco de Coronado and his men trekked in a vain search for gold in 1540. The area offers trout fishing, big game hunting, rock hunting, hiking, riding, camping, picnicking, outstanding scenic panoramas, Mogollon Rim, sportsmen's lodges, meadow, pine and aspen forests, streams, nearby Indian ruins, ghost towns and wildlife.

Tucson

CACTUS FOREST LOOP DRIVE is in Saguaro National Monument (15 miles west of Tucson) and features one of the densest stands of Saguaro cactus in the world, as well as other desert species.

HITCHCOCK HIGHWAY, up Mt. Lemmon, northeast of Tucson, includes very impressive scenic views, Rose Lake, national forest camp and picnic sites, outdoor recreation and nature walks.

KITT PEAK, 45 miles southwest of the city off Highway 86, offers fine birds-eye views of the vast Papago Indian Reservation, cattle ranches, mountain-streaked deserts, forest picnic areas, and Kitt Peak National Observatory.

PIONEER PARKWAY (US 89 northward) crosses through one of the state's best natural desert gardens. Tucson Mountain Park roads west of the city offer breathtaking desert vistas.

Walpi

The road from Polacca to First Mesa is narrow, twistng and scary—but safe—and leads to Mano, Sichomovi and Walpi. You can park at the first two villages and walk the rest of the way to meet Hopi people, see their homes, and look out on vast stretches of the Indian reservation and the San Francisco Peaks in the distance.

Williams

Bill Williams Mountain south of town has a good road leading to its summit, where travelers can look northward to the Grand Canyon and take in vast panoramas of northern Arizona.

Yarnell

US 89, just south of town, offers numerous beautiful views as it climbs Yarnell Hill to a lookout point far above the desert regions stretched out below.

CHAPTER 2

GHOST TOWNS

Arizona's ghost towns are shadowy reminders of pioneer settlements and once-thriving communities; towns from the late 19th Century that did not survive the boom-to-bust cycle. In the beginning, these relics were mill towns, mining camps, smelting towns and centers of commerce.

Vicissitudes in mining and changes in the water supply left these ghosts of towns scattered all over the map of Arizona.

In 1849 thousands of prospectors from California headed for Arizona. They traveled east, crossing the Colorado River, in the hope of finding the great wealth that eluded them in the Golden State. The Gadsen Purchase some four years later opened up the land below the Gila River, a land rich in resources. In 1858 traces of gold was discovered along the Gila River. This discovery triggered Arizona's first Gold Rush. Miners and speculators swarmed into the area, shifting their attention from silver to gold. Gila City was born in this hectic age, falling ultimately into disuse once the ore was exhausted.

The dry Arizona air has preserved enough ghost towns to satisfy those who seek adventure and exploration. This is especially true for anyone who likes to poke around crumbling stage stations, dust-covered mine shafts, assay offices, slag piles and musty, abandoned saloons.

After the Civil War, copper and silver were pursued by the most avid prospectors. Gold did not return to prominence until about 1890.

SOUTHEASTERN ARIZONA

Courtland

One-time thriving mining camp named for Courtland Young, mining engineer. Only things remaining are two buildings, a jail and a lone hostile inhabitant. In Cochise County, 21 miles north of Douglas, off US 666.

Dos Cabezas

Semi-ghost town where a few residents still live, supporting a small post office. Formally an active supply center for surrounding mines and cattle ranches. Crumbling adobe ruins. In Cochise County on Route 186, 15 miles southeast of Willcox.

Duquesne

A mining camp at the turn of the century, it is now almost all ruins. Had a peak population of 1,000 residents, including Westinghouse of Westinghouse Electric, who lived here while taking four million dollars in ore from his nearby mine. In Santa Cruz County, 19 miles east of Nogales.

Gleeson

Here the Indians mined turquoise before the arrival of the Spaniards. Mining town for copper, lead and zinc. Fire destroyed the town in 1912. In Cochise County, 16 miles east of Tombstone.

Mowry

Small town which grew up around an old silver, lead and zinc mine. Purchased in the late 1850's. Had a population of 500 at its peak. Deserted buildings and cemetery remain. In Santa Cruz County, 15 miles southeast of Patagonia.

Oro Blanco

Once the home of James A. Robinson, the richest man in Arizona. $1,130,000 in gold was taken from this locality between 1873 and 1932. Adobe ruins. In Santa Cruz County, 20 miles west of Nogales.

Pearce

Discovered by a man named Pearce in 1894. In its heyday the Old Commonwealth was the richest gold digging in Southern Arizona. Many vacant adobes, mines and mill ruins. In Cochise County, 1 mile off US 66 from a point 29 miles south of Willcox.

Sunnyside

A unique mining town - a religious cooperative community. Operated Copper Glance Mine. Bible reading was the rule; no drinking or prostitution like other mining towns. Leave Sierra Vista going south on State Highway 92.

Washington Camp

Once a major service community for Duquesne, Mowry and Harshaw. In 1905 it had a population of 5,200 miners and their families. In Santa Cruz County, 20 miles south of Patagonia.

WEST CENTRAL ARIZONA

Goldroad

Gold was discovered here in 1864. In 1949 most of remaining mining operations and buildings were razed to escape taxes. Now mostly diggings and minor ruins. In Mohave County, 23 miles southeast of Kingman.

Oatman

A small number of residents remain here so it is not a 100% Ghost Town. But it is a popular site for tourists, photographers and rockhounds. See directions on how to get to Goldroad above.

Signal

Established in the late 1870's as a mining town for ore from McCrackin and Signal Mines. In it's heydey it had stores, shops and hotels. An old saloon, a cemetery and an adobe ruin mark the site. In Mohave County, 60 miles northwest of Wickenburg.

Swansea

Founded at the turn of the century. Swansea headquarters of the Clara Consolidated Gold and Copper Mining Company. Once had a population of 750. To get there ask for specific directions in Parker.

MID-CENTRAL ARIZONA

Congress

Site of the wealthy Congress Gold Mine. Ruins of old cabins and rubble-strewn flats. Old cemetery is well maintained. Yavapai County, approximately 2 miles from Congress Junction.

Stanton

This town owed its name to the selfish ambition of entrepreneur Charles P. Stanton. He kept a store and stage station and was also Postmaster in 1875. Later this community became an active mining camp. In Yavapai County, 6 miles east of Arrowhead Station on US 89; 42 miles southwest of Prescott.

Weaver

A picturesque town named after Pauline Weaver, a famous mountain man and guide, whose party accidently discovered a rich gold strike. The site was called "Rich Hill." A tent city sprang up overnight after the discovery. A cemetery and several adobe ruins remain. In Yavapai County, 4 miles southeast of Stanton.

EAST CENTRAL ARIZONA

McMillanville

Supported by the celebrated Stonewall Jackson Mine. Discovered in 1876. Produced some $3 million in silver during its operation. The silver was discovered by accident. However, by 1885 all the ore was exhausted. Only scattered ruins remain. In Gila County, near US 60, about 10 miles northeast of Globe.

NORTHWESTERN ARIZONA

White Hills

In the 1890's this was a rowdy silver camp between Globe and Virginia City. In a brief 6 years the 15 forgotten mines which surrounded it, gave up $12,000,000 in silver bullion. In 1895 an English firm assumed ownership of the mine and provided such amenities as running water, electric lights and telephones. A short time later the ore was nonexistent and the mines were abandoned. In Mohave County, 50 miles north of Kingman, off route 93.

Jerome: The living Ghost Town

Jerome is one of the most unusual places to visit in the entire West. It has gravitated from prosperous mining town to ghost town to an art/craft/retirement center.

In 1876 as a result of the filing of the first mineral claim, the town mushroomed. Jerome had a population of 15,000 at one time. Early settlers lived in crude shacks and tents, then impressive homes, hotels and other buildings turned the mining camp into a thriving town. But changing technologies, smelting inefficiency and finally the Great Depression of the 1930's and depletion of the ore, doomed the famous town. A mass exodus took place. However, a few hardy, determined souls stayed on and kept Jerome alive. In 1967, the town was declared a National Historic Landmark.

There is lots to see in and around Jerome: old houses on stilts, a once-thriving hotel called the "The Montana," homes of native stone, old schools, a Mining Museum* and a State Park. Main Street is now quite active with tourists shopping and browsing in a variety of places that offer antiques, jewelry, art work and clothing.

The town is snuggled on the precipitous slopes of Cleopatra Hill above 5,000 feet, offering a panoramic view of the beautiful Verde Valley, the redrock country of Sedona and the distant San Francisco Peaks. Not bad for nature lovers and camera buffs!

Jerome is located on Highway 89A between Flagstaff and Prescott.

•

***Museum charges an admission.**

CHAPTER 3

TOWN DAYS, PARADES & RODEOS

Arizona is alive with year-around parades, Town Days, rodeos, festivals, fairs and celebrations of many kinds. They occur in every region of the state and in every season. Many are free. A number of rodeos have been left out of this listing because they charge admission.

Events and celebrations are sometimes held on different dates. For current information, contact the local Chamber of Commerce where you plan to visit.
(See the back of this book for addresses and phone numbers of Arizona Chambers of Commerce.)

CENTRAL ARIZONA

Apache Junction

Lost Dutchman Days - Last weekend in January.
Commemorates the legendary Lost Dutchman Mines that countless bounty seekers have searched for over the years. Key event is a 2-hour parade, floats, art show and entertainment.

Cave Creek

Cave Creek Craft Fall Festival - End of November
Annual Cave Creek Christmas Pageant - Mid-December
Desert Foothills Fiesta Day & Parade - Early April
Cave Creek Council Spring Festival - Early April

Fountain Hills

Women's Club House Walk - Late November

Gilbert

Gilbert Days - Late November, weekend prior to Thanksgiving. A parade and downtown activities.

Glendale

Thunderbird International Hot Air Balloon Race - Mid-November
Balloon accuracy races, concessions, displays. Very colorful event.

Greer

Greer Days - Early June
Two days of special activities.

Jerome

Annual Jerome Theme & Memorabilia Show - Month of August

Mesa

Tag-a-long Tours of City - April to July
Unique, no-cost walking tours of key historic and archeological sights; also some good nature study tours.

Gold Rush Western Days - Early October

Payson

Rodeo Parade - Early March
Town goes all out to make visitors happy. One of the better rodeo parades held in the state.

Prescott

Cinco De Mayo Parade - Early May
Parade honoring famous Mexican holiday.

Prescott Valley Days - Late June
Prescott's version of Western Town Day.

Frontier Days Parade - July 4th celebration

Phoenix

Rodeo of Rodeos Parade - March
One of the most publicized and well attended parades in the West. Exciting, worth seeing. Local media in Phoenix give the exact route and hours.

Hello Phoenix - Late March at Civic Center, downtown Phoenix. This is the closest event that Phoenix has to a Town Day. It is a celebration of the city's ethnic diversity. Arts & crafts, ethnic displays, foods, entertainment.

Cinco De Mayo Parades - Early May
Check local neighborhood for celebration of this Mexican holiday.

Fiesta Bowl Parade - Mid-December
Full of color and excitement, this parade gets bigger and better every year. It is held to celebrate the now famous Fiesta Bowl which is played at Sun Devil Stadium, the home of Arizona State University's football team in Tempe.

Scottsdale

Parada Del Sol - Late January or early March
Reputation for one of the finest parades in the Valley of the Sun at any time. This is the longest horse drawn parade in the U.S.

Sedona

Christmas Tree Lighting Ceremony at Chamber of Commerce -Early December

Festival of Lights at Tlaquepaque (a unique shopping area) -Early December

Annual St. Patrick's Day Parade - Late March
This St. Patrick's Day Parade has a Western flavor. Very enjoyable with marching bands, locally sponsored motorized displays.

Tempe

Fireworks Displays - Various locations - July 4th

Wickenburg

Gold Rush Days - Mid-February
Well planned events include free shows, gem and mineral displays, arts & crafts and a parade.

Fireworks Display - July 4th

NORTHERN ARIZONA

Holbrook

Navajo County Fair - Dates change. Best to contact Chamber of Commerce. Fair events include rodeo, horse show and entertainment.

Pinetop
Fall Festival Parade - Late September

St. Johns
Apache County Fair
4-H Fair, Horse Show and Sale
St. Johns Parade - Late July

Show Low
Town Events - July 4th
Parade, picnicking, fireworks display, contests, prizes.

Winslow
Annual Christmas Parade - Late December

SOUTHERN ARIZONA

Bisbee
Annual Parade - July 4th

La Vuelta de Bisbee
Bicycle races with the atmosphere of a Town Day

Brewery Gulch Days - Labor Day weekend
Town is decked out. Mostly an arts & craft show.

Duncan
Greenlee County Fair - Early October
Features rodeo, horse show, dog show and entertainment.

Nogales
Christmas Parade - Early December

Sierra Vista
Annual Coronado Historical Pageant - April

Annual Huachuca Mountain Stampede Days - Early May

Annual City Celebration - July 4th

Safford
Annual Celebration - July 4th

WESTERN ARIZONA

Kingman

VFW Loyalty Day Parade - Early May

Fireworks Display - July 4th

Andy Devine Days - Early October
Kingman is the boyhood home of this one-time famous movie star. The day is in his honor.

Lake Havasu City

London Bridge Days - Late September - Early October
Celebrates the dedication of this world-famous bridge at this Arizona city in 1971. It was removed from London, England to this spot and placed here. There are lots of English costumes in evidence, contests, music and a special parade.

Oatman

Old Timers Day - Late May
Reunion of old timers from the area; photo display, story telling, make-believe gunfights and music.

Page

Old Fashioned 4th - July 4th
Parades, games, music.

Here Comes Santa Claus Parade - First Saturday in December

Parker

National Indian Celebration - September
Authentic Indian dances performed by tribes from many different areas of the United States. Miss Colorado River Indian Reservation leads a parade. Free barbeque, exhibits, contests and awards.

Old West Daze Parade - Mid-October
There's a Rodeo Queen, drill teams, floats from various local businesses and clubs.

Tucson Area

For a complete listing of the several hundred events of a cultural, entertainment and educational nature that are held in and near Tucson each year, contact the Tucson Convention & Visitors Bureau in Placita Village, 350 S. Church, downtown. Telephone 791-4768

Mexican Independence Day - Observed at Nogales, Mexico, 65 miles south of Tucson, on September 16, this is a major Mexican festival and includes a parade, colorful floats, street dancing and much merry making. Well worth the drive to the shop-filled border town.

Feast of St. Francis of Assisi - A candlelight procession at night is one of the highlights of this annual early October event, held at the famous San Xavier Mission church nine miles outside of Tucson. For the exact date and best time to go, call 294-0628

Helldorado Days - Residents of Tombstone, 73 miles southeast of Tucson, re-enact some of the most famous events in the history of "The Town Too Tough To Die" including the Gunfight at O.K. Corral. Begins on the third Friday in October and lasts thru Sunday.

Papago Indian Fair - This is the biggest event of the year for Tucson's Papago Indian neighbors. It is held at Sells, the Papago's tribal headquarters, about 62 miles west of Tucson, around November 20-21. The fair gate opens at 10 a.m. The rodeo portion of the festivities begins at 1 p.m.

Inter-Collegiate Championship Rodeo - Sponsored by the University of Arizona and held at the Tucson Rodeo Grounds on about November 8-9, this event attracts college students from throughout the West.

St. Xavier Fiesta - Fireworks, Indian dancing and a procession at the beautiful San Xavier Mission honor the church's patron saint.

Tucson Square Dance Festival - Square dancers, callers and fans gather from all over the country for this colorful annual event. It is held in late January. Call the Tucson Chamber of Commerce for the exact date and place, 792-1212.

Arizona State Trapshoot Meet - Held at the Tucson Trap and Skeet Club, 7800 W. Ajo Way, in January. Call for time and details. Telephone 883-6426.

Tubac Festival of Arts & Crafts - Forty four miles south of Tucson on the Nogales Highway. Tubac was the location of the first American community established in what is now Arizona. It was an important Spanish fort for nearly 100 years. It is now a popular retirement community and a center for arts and crafts. The annual festival is held the first or second week of February.

All States Picnic - Tucson's annual "All States' Picnic" is attended by thousands of winter visitors and Southern Arizonans who migrated from other states. Call 792-1212 for time and place.

Tucson Gem & Mineral Show - Held each year at the Tucson Community Center Exhibit Hall (350 S. Church Street, downtown) in mid-February, this 3-day event is regarded by most afficionados as the best in the world. It includes exhibits, demonstrations, programs by eminent minerologists and hobbyists, and selected wholesaler and retailer displays from around the world. For more information contact the Tucson Gem & Mineral Committee, Box 6363, Tucson, AZ 85733.

La Fiesta de los Vaqueros - This is the largest and most colorful annual event in Tucson. The four-day celebration includes rodeos, parades, carnival-type entertainment and numerous other fun activities. Begins about February 20th.

Aerospace and Arizona Days - Military displays, air shows and drill competition at Davis-Monthan Air Force Base adjoining Tucson on the southeast, in mid-March. There is no charge, and refreshments are available.

Pima County Fair - A 5-day County Fair and Livestock Show, held at the new Fairgrounds on Houghton Road, one mile south of Interstate 10 (the Freeway), from 10 a.m. to 10 p.m. daily. Activities include horse shows, livestock sales, displays of all kinds, side-shows, rides, cotton candy, etc. There is a nominal admission charge, Call the Tucson Chamber of Commerce for this year's dates.—792-1212.

Yaqui Indian Ceremonies - Exotic "Holy Week" (March 19-26) ceremonials held by the Yaqui Indians near New Pascua Village, Calle Central, south of Grant Road. Visitors are welcome at the festivities, but are not allowed to take pictures.

Tucson Festival Week - A series of events designed to perpetuate Tucson's History and cultural past are staged from around April 4 thru 11. These include: San Xavier Fiesta; La Fiesta de las Flores; Festival Art Show; La Parada de los Ninos; La Fiesta de la Placia; and the Pioneer Jubilee.

Cinco de Mayo Celebration in Nogales - This 5th of May celebration is another of Mexico's major holidays, and it is marked in Nogales with great gusto. There are parades, floats, dancing, fireworks, music and merry-making in general.

VISITING MEXICO

Nogales, Mexico is only a 90-minute drive from Tucson. If you plan on going beyond this border city, you will need a "Tourist Card" (similar to a visa), which can be obtained free of charge at

Mexico's "Tourism Plaza," 2744 E. Broadway in Tucson, while you wait.

In addition to the Gov't Tourism Office that issues tourist cards, the Plaza has a Mexican insurance company (Mexican auto insurance is essential if you are going to drive into the interior of the country); a travel service; an agency that operates caravans into and from Mexico; a Mexican handicraft shop, and a Mexican Restaurant.

When applying for a Tourist Card you must present one of the following kinds of identification: birth certificate; voter's registration card; passport; military I.D. that shows place of birth; a typed notorized affidavit stating your name, place of birth and citizenship.

CHAPTER 4

HISTORIC SITES

Arizona boasts over 10,000 years of Indian, Spanish, Mexican and American influences. Granted statehood in 1912, Arizona has evolved as a result of a mixed bag of races and origins.

During the 1820's and 1830's, Americans began to explore Arizona. For 25 years after Mexico won independence from Spain (1821), Arizona was part of the Republic of Mexico. The Mexican War of 1846 was won by the United States under President Polk. The Treaty of Guadalupe Hidalgo in 1848 defined the area North of the Gila River as U.S. Territory. In addition, the Gadsen Purchase of 1854 gave the United States the area south of the Gila River, including the city of Tucson.

However, it was not until 1863 that Arizona was granted official U. S. Territorial status. Prior to this recognition, Arizona was just an isolated land mass in the Territory of New Mexico.

The Historic Sites in Arizona illustrate the evolution and development of this most beautiful state.

SOUTHEASTERN ARIZONA

Coronado National Monument

Commemorates the first European exploration into what is now the United States by Francisco Vasquez de Coronado. It is situated on the boundary of the United States and Mexico. Location: Cochise County, 30 miles southwest of Bisbee via Arizona 92 and secondary road.

Ft. Bowie National Historic Site

Located on the homeland of the Chiricahua Apache Indians. During the Civil War, California volunteers established the Fort. Later, famous Indian Chiefs such as Geronimo, Cochise and others, spread warfare throughout the southwest. The army abandoned the site in 1894 after the Indian Wars were over. In Cochise County, thirteen miles south of Bowie.

Lehner Mammoth-Kill Site

This site dates back to 11,000 B.C., and is an outstanding example of other such structures found elsewhere in the New World. The well-preserved site has revealed stone butchery tools with fluted spear points. Location: 10 miles west of Bisbee.

Tombstone Historic District

Perhaps the most famous gunbattle of all times took place here in 1881 near the now-famous O.K. Corral. Note the genuine Western frontier flavor of the Bird Cage Theatre, City Hall, St. Paul's Episcopal Church and the County Court House. Only the County Court House has been designated a state historic park. See Chapter 9 on State Parks. Location: In Cochise County, off Arizona 82, some 69 miles from Tucson.

Fremont House

A splendid example of an adobe residence built around the year 1870, common at that time in Tucson. Named for the Territorial Governor of Arizona. Location: In downtown Tucson.

Old Adobe Patio

Part of the Charles O. Brown House. Brown made a success of his Congress Street Saloon and other Tucson enterprises. His first home was the Mexican territorial style structure at the south end of the patio facing Jackson Street. Location: In downtown Tucson.

San Xavier Del Bac

This magnificent Spanish Colonial church, often called "The White Dove of the Desert," was begun in 1700. It is constructed of brick covered with stucco and has a baroque style interior, richly ornamented. It is considered the finest example of mission architecture in the United States. Location: On the Papago Indian Reservation some 9 miles south of Tucson via Mission Road.

Tucson Museum of Art Complex

This complex occupies the northern section of the old Tucson Presidio. Check out the *Fish House* and *Stevens House,* both steeped in the local history of 19th century Tucson and excellent examples of the architecture of the same period. Part of the complex includes *La Casa Cordoba,* believed to be the oldest surviving structure in Tucson. It has been continuously inhabited by Mexican families. Recently restored as a Mexican Heritage Museum.

Don't pass up the *Leonardo Romero House,* built about 1868, now part of the Tucson Museum of Art School. Location: Downtown Tucson.

Vantana Cave

Famous for its possible 5,000 years of continuous occupation by Arizona Indians. The cave is high and shallow and lies at the base of a cliff. Location: In Pima County, 11 miles west of Santa Rosa on the Papago Indian Reservation.

Calabasa

Started as a Pima Indian village and missionary site in the 18th century. Apache raids forced abandonment of the village in 1783. Ruins of remodeled church, circa 1844. Location: In Santa Cruz County, north of Nogales.

Tumacacori National Monument

Jesuit priests established this old mission of San Jose de Tumacacori during the 17th century. It flowered between 1790 and 1821 with the spread of Christianity into what is now the American southwest. Location: 18 miles north of Nogales on Interstate 19.

Tubac Presidio

See Chapter 9 on State Parks. At various times in the state's history, Tubac was its most important town. In 1770 it was at Tubac that the Spanish northward drive was halted. Location: Broadway and River Road, Tubac.

SOUTHWESTERN ARIZONA

Old La Paz

The town flourished as a gold center and river port for about seven years. Between 1862 and 1873, La Paz had over 5,000 residents. The course of the Colorado River shifted in 1870, leaving La Paz two miles inland. Location: Yuma County, 8 miles north of Ehrenberg on the Colorado River Indian Reservation.

Mohave Indian Presbyterian Church

This old adobe building, measuring 43 by 24 feet, has served as a religious center for Mohave Indians since just before World War I. Location: Southwest of Parker on 2nd Avenue.

Yuma Crossing

During the Spanish colonial period this was a means of transportation and communication between Alta California and New Spain. See State Park Chapter for more information on the Arizona Territorial Prison in Yuma. Location: In Yuma, directly on the Colorado River.

WEST CENTRAL ARIZONA

Fortaleza

Unique ruins. Site believed to have been constructed by Hohokam Indians during the 14th century. Location: In Maricopa County, near Gila Bend.

Gatlin Site

Archeologists believe that this was a ceremonial structure used by Hohokam Indians. Still visible are the ball court and trash mound. Location: In Maricopa County, 3 miles north of Gila Bend.

Camp Beale Springs

The Fort, established in 1871, was named for a Lt. Beale who once used camels on his expeditions while mapping a wagon road. Remains include foundations of 10 adobe and three frame buildings. Location: In the vicinity of Kingman, Fort Beale Drive and Wagon Trail Road.

MID-CENTRAL ARIZONA

Walnut Canyon National Monument

Ruins of over 300 small cliff dwellings. Inhabitants lived during the Stone Age and probably chose the site for its available water and protection. Location: 8 miles east of Flagstaff via US 66.

Wupatki National Monument

Agricultural Indians built these red sandstone pueblos. Within the vast area, there are over 800 ruins. Location: 30 miles north of Flagstaff off US 89.

Roosevelt Dam

World's highest masonry dam, 284 feet high and 1,125 feet long. Provides water storage for the Salt River Irrigation Complex. Location: On the Salt River, 31 miles northwest of Globe on Arizona 88.

Tonto National Monument

Built during the 1300's and considered one of the best cliff dwellings in Arizona. The dwellings have masonry walls and mud roofs. The theory is that skilled artisans lived here and produced such things as highly decorative and attractive pottery. Location: 28 miles northwest of Globe on Arizona 88.

Arizona State Capitol Building

Added to the National Register of Historic Sites in the mid 1970's. Built in 1897, it has a low central dome set in an octogonal base. It is a "must see" tourist attraction if you are visiting Phoenix. Location: In downtown Phoenix at 1700 W. Washington Street.

Phoenix Carnegie Library

This neo-classical, one story brick structure is right in downtown Phoenix. Built in 1908, it was the result of a grant by Andrew Carnegie. Location: 1101 W. Washington Street.

Roy Hackett House

Built in 1888, this was once a one-story bakery. Remodeled in 1906. Location: 401 and 405 Maple Streets, in Tempe.

Tuzigoot National Monument

Hohokam Indians constructed this almost 100-room hilltop pueblo around 1000 A.D. Museum now stores a collection of artifacts discovered during the excavation in 1933. Location: Yavapai County, 2 miles east of Clarkdale.

EAST CENTRAL ARIZONA

Point of Pines Sites

First occupants of the Indian village date back to around 2000 B.C. Famous for large excavated pueblo (800 rooms). Quite unusual. Location: 30 miles northwest of Morenci on the San Carlos Indian Reservation.

Kearny Campsite and Trail

Named for General Stephen Watts Kearny who camped here in 1846. It marks the most difficult part of his journey from Sante Fe to California along the Gila River. Added recently to the National Register of Historic Sites. Location: Northeast of Safford, off US 666.

Kinishba Ruins

Arizona Indians settled here sometime in the 1300's. The site lasted about 100 years and produced skilled examples of pottery. Location: 15 miles west of White River via Arizona 73 and secondary road.

NORTHEASTERN ARIZONA

Navajo National Monument

One of the most famous of prehistoric cliff dwellings. The "Betatkin" cliff dwelling contained 100 rooms and was 450 feet long. Location: 30 miles southwest of Kayenta on the Navajo Indian Reservation.

Avatori Ruins

Spanish explorers reached the Hopi village about 1540. Christianity was taught by missionaries, but in 1700 Avatori was destroyed by neighboring villages that resented the new religious teachings. Location: 8 miles south of Keams Canyon on the Hopi Indian Reservation.

Old Oraibi

This is the oldest inhabited pueblo in the southwest. It has 13 Kivas, 7 discontinuous houses. Very important site for students of prehistoric pueblo culture in Arizona. Location: 3 miles west of Oraibi on Arizona 264, inside the Hopi Indian Reservation.

Canyon De Chelly National Monument

Spectacular prehistoric dwellings situated both in caves and at the base of steep cliffs in one of Arizona's most spectacular canyons. Valuable artifacts have been almost miraculously preserved, due to Arizona's arid climate. See some of the more important specific sites, such as Antelope House, White House and Mummy Cave Ruin. Location: At the east side of Chinle on the Navajo Indian Reservation.

Hubbell Trading Post

This is the oldest surviving trading post of its kind. Founded in 1876 by Don Lorenzo Hubbell on the Navajo Indian Reservation. Has served to revive traditional and much-in-demand Navajo rug weaving. Location: On the west side of Ganado on the Navajo Indian Reservation.

James M. Flake House

This 2½ story brick house was built in 1896 and served as a rest stop for Mormons trekking across the country from the midwest. Interesting Queen Anne decorative elements. Location: Stinson and Hunt Streets in the downtown area of Snowflake.

Jesse N. Smith

Built for a bishop in the Mormon church. In 1906 when the house was completed, it stood as a symbol of Mormon pioneer determination and spirit. Location: 203 W. Smith Avenue in Snowflake.

NORTHWESTERN ARIZONA

El Tovar Hotel

Charles Whittlesey, an architect, built this historic hotel in 1905. It is a 3-story structure made of logs, stone, frame and clapboarding. Location: Route 8A in the Grand Canyon National Park.

Grand Canyon Railroad Station

Was built in 1898 to serve a copper mine in the area. However, it became more famous for train passenger service to the Grand Canyon (which ended in 1968). See the quaint log Station House. Location: Route 8A in the Grand Canyon National Park.

Grandview Mine

Ruins of a once operating mine. It started in 1892, but closed in 1907. Only a few things remain, including a shanty, some mining equipment and a mine shaft. Location: In Grand Canyon National Park.

Superintendent's Residence

First administrative headquarters of Grand Canyon National Park, built in 1921. Remodeled and enlarged in 1931. Location: Off route 8A in Grand Canyon National Park.

Tusayan Ruins

1200 A.D. Indian ruins. Remains of U-shaped pueblo with two round kivas and a two-story living quarter. Good example of Anasazi Indian culture. Location: On the southern border of Grand Canyon National Monument.

Pipe Spring National Monument

Mormon missionaries and pioneers explored the area near this century fort in 1858. By 1869 the Mormon Church bought the land, then built a ranch with a defensive fort. Monument contains soldier's quarters, two red-stoned fort structures and a spring. Location: 15 miles southwest of Fredonia, off US 389.

CHAPTER 5

VISITING ARIZONA'S INDIAN COUNTRY

One of Arizona's greatest attractions is its *Indian Country* -over 20 Reservations totaling 19½ million acres (comprising 27 percent of the state's land mass), which boasts the largest Indian population in the United States.

In most cases, the Reservations represent the traditional homelands of Arizona's 14 Indian tribes, and range from the desert lands of Central, South and Southwestern Arizona to the spectacular mountain and canyon areas of the state's North and Northeastern regions.

In his highly informative book, *Visitor's Guide to Arizona's Indian Reservations,** author Boye De Mente tells how Arizona's Indians survived to become one of the state's primary resources:". . . the Indians of Arizona for nearly 100 years were on the verge of suffering the same fate as the Mohawks, the Mohicans, the Powhatan, the Seneca, dozens of other tribes, and the buffalo- . . . but the wild ruggedness of the territory's great mountains, plateaus and canyons of the Northern and Eastern areas and the dry cactus-studded deserts of the Central and Southern portion kept American settlers and soldiers out of Arizona until quite late in the western movement of the country . . ."

Several of the larger Reservations (Fort Apache in the White Mountains, the Navajo and Hopi Reservations in particular) have well developed and thriving tourist industries. All except the tiniest of the Reservations have their own distinctive attractions

---

***Visitor's Guide to Arizona's Indian Reservations* is available from Phoenix Books/Publishers, POB 32008, Phoenix, Arizona 85064 USA. $3.95 pp.**

that make up some of the unique experiences available free to Arizona residents and visitors.

Some of the tribes still practice ancient religious ceremonies that are off limits to visitors, although visitors are invited to view some portions of these ceremonies as well. The famous *kivas,* or underground ceremonial chambers of the Hopi tribe, are permanently taboo to outsiders.

In all instances, visitors to Arizona's Indian Country are expected to behave as considerate guests who respect the privacy and rights of their hosts.

LOCATION OF THE INDIAN RESERVATIONS

Central Arizona

Campe Verde: This is the state's smallest reservations with only 578 acres. It is located in the geographic center of the state, approximately 80 miles from Flagstaff, south on I-17

Fort Apache: Covers over 1,650,000 acres, dotted with forests, lakes and mountains; it is a mecca for summer vacationers. Several areas still reflect the Apache way of life. About 8 miles south of Whiteriver on State Highway 73.

Gila Bend Indian Reservation: Is southwest of Phoenix, off State Highway 85 and encompassing 10,297 acres. It is the home of the Maricopa Indians, who are famous for a variety of pottery.

Gila River Indian Reservation: Comprises 371,929 acres and is an easy drive from Phoenix on State Route 87 and other roads. Sacaton is the tribal headquarters, with Pima Indians in the majority.

Maricopa: The area, just south of Phoenix, comprises some 21,840 acres. The customs of the Maricopa are close to the ways of the Pima. They are also known for their good pottery.

Salt River Indian Reservation: This reservation is just east of Scottsdale, very accessible to visitors to the Valley of the Sun. It has over 46,590 acres. Most of the work performed by the Indians on the reservation is agricultural in nature.

San Carlos Indian Reservation: Near Globe, this reservation is huge - some 1,854,801 acres. The Indians raise cattle as a primary industry. One popular event on the reservation is the well-known *Apache Devil Dance.* The tribe is respected for their basket-making.

Northeast Area of the State

Hopi Indian Reservation: North of Winslow, this is the most unusual of all the Indian Reservations. Villages in this huge 2,472,216 acre land mass are mostly located atop high mesas. Oraibi, one of these villages, is believed to have originated around 1200 A.D. Here on this big reservation the visitor can buy silver, jewelry, weaving, basketry, pottery and Kachina dolls. Some old ceremonial functions are still practiced, such as the primitive Annual Snake Dance.

Kaibab Indian Reservation: This reservation is near the Arizona-Utah border and comprises about 120,400 acres. It is the home for the Paiute Indians, famous for their special craft item called the "wedding basket."

Navajo Indian Reservation: This sprawling 25,000 square mile reservation is the largest and most scenic of all Indian reservations. It is situated in the northeastern corner of the state with Window Rock as its picturesque capital. The Navajo territory, which extends into Utah and New Mexico, includes such diverse towns as Tuba City, Ft. Defiance, Kayenta and others. It is a domain of desert, canyons, red rocks and pinion tree (dwarf pine trees). Navajo's excel at weaving and are good silversmiths. Look for the famous Navajo houses, called "hogans." These forked-stick and six-sided homes are made of logs, and are symbolic of the Navajo Indian. Some of the Navajo still lead semi-nomadic lives, guiding sheep to grazing lands. It is such a vast land that someone has called it: "Land of Room Enough and Time Enough."

Near Grand Canyon

Havasupai Indian Reservation: This 188,0777 site, north of US 66, has been called "The Land of the Blue-Green Waters," or simply a "Shangri-La." There are three spectacular waterfalls on the reservation that draw tourists every season. But a visit to the small headquarter village of Supai is a must. It is set in a deep canyon, a unique place to view, with peach orchards, horse corrals, gardens and old traditional houses that resist the march of the 20th century. It is necessary to plan in advance if you want to visit the Havasupai Indian Reservation. Access into the reservation is not easy; although there are heliocopter tours for a fee. Facilities such as lodges are extremely limited. For more information and reservations, write to: Havasupai Tourist Enterprises, Supai, Arizona 86435, Phone: 448-2121.

Southern Arizona

Papago Indian Reservation: It is situated between Tucson and Ajo - another huge area of some 2,773,000 acres. Indian homes here include mud, adobe and wattle structures as well as modern frame houses. The Indians on the reservation are engaged in farming and raising cattle. Basketmaking is the leading handicraft.

San Xavier Indian Reservation: This over 71,000 acre reservation is just southwest of Tucson. It is, as its name implies, around the Mission San Xavier del Bac. The Indian residents are part of the Papago tribe.

Other Regions: Parker & Yuma

Cocopa Indian Reservation: This reservation covers only 528 acres near Yuma. It is the home of a small tribe devoted to farming.

Colorado River Indian Reservation: This Indian Reservation is just south of Parker, along the Colorado River. It contains over 225,000 acres. Emphasis here is on water sports and a thriving agriculture.

DEER TRACK . . . . . . Plenty Game
BEAR TRACK . . . . . . Good Omen
RATTLESNAKE JAW . . . . . Strength
HEADDRESS . . . . Ceremonial Dance
BUTTERFLY . . . . Everlasting Life
COYOTE TRACKS
TEPEE . . . . . . Temporary Home
SKY BAND . . . . Leading to Happiness
MEDICINE MAN'S EYE . . . . Wise, Watchful
MOUNTAIN RANGE
HOGAN . . . . . . Permanent Home
BIG MOUNTAIN . . . . . Abundance

RAIN CLOUDS . . . . Good Prospects

LIGHTNING AND LIGHTNING ARROW . . . Swiftness

DAYS AND NIGHTS . . . . . . Time

MORNING STARS . . . . . Guidance

SUN SYMBOLS . . . . . Happiness

RUNNING WATER . . . . Constant Life

RAINDROP — RAIN . . Plentiful Crops

HORSE . . . . . . Journey

THUNDERBIRD . . . . Sacred Bearer of Happiness Unlimited

CROSSED ARROWS . . . . Friendship

ARROW . . . . Protection

ARROWHEAD . . . . Alertness

4 AGES . . . . . Infancy, Youth, Middle and Old Age

CACTUS . . . . . Sign of the Desert

GILA MONSTER . . . Sign of the Desert

CACTUS FLOWER . . . . . . Courtship

HOUSE OF WATER

FENCE . . . . Guarding Good Luck

ENCLOSURE FOR CEREMONIAL DANCES

EAGLE FEATHERS . . . . Chief

WARDING OFF EVIL SPIRITS

PATHS CROSSING

PEACE

MAN . . . . . Human Life

BIRD . . . . Carefree — Lighthearted

LIGHTNING SNAKE

SNAKE . . . . . . Defiance, Wisdom

THUNDERBIRD TRACK Bright Prospects

SUN RAYS . . . Constancy

LASSO . . . . . . Captivity

SADDLE BAGS . . . . Journey

CHAPTER 6

ARTS & CRAFTS MUSEUMS

One of the country's youngest states, Arizona has much to offer in art and craft relics from the past. Perhaps because of the state's favorable climate, objects are dug up in better condition than in most other parts of the world. Relics have been found throughout the entire state. A few such collections are not only varied and beautiful, but also unique.

Arizona History Room

Located in the lobby of First Interstate Bank, First Avenue and Washington. Collection of old maps, gold nuggets, old weapons and photos of Arizona's beginnings. Open 10 a.m. to 3 p.m. on weekdays only.

Arizona Historical Society

Phoenix Chapter at 1242 N. Central Avenue. Museum features history of Phoenix and Central Arizona. Has costume gallery, old-time pharmacy and a "touch museum" for children. Open Tuesday-Saturday 10 a.m. to 4 p.m.

Arizona Mineral Museum

State Fairgrounds at McDowell and 19th Avenue. Great collection of all kinds of Arizona's ores and minerals. There is a fluorescent display as well as exhibits on earth sciences. Hours: 9 a.m. to 5 p.m. Monday to Friday; Saturday and Sunday Noon to 4 p.m.

Arizona State Capital Museum

Washington and 17th Avenue, on the third floor. Several murals depict the state's history. Also, Indian artifacts, documents, relics and portraits of former governors of the State.

University (ASU) Art Collections

Located at Matthews Center on the campus of Arizona State University in Tempe. Has fine collection of American paintings -one of the best from an historical point of view. All the paintings are from West of the Mississippi. Also has a good collection of sculptures, prints and folk art.

Pueblo Grande Museum

4619 E. Washington. One of the best museums of its kind in Arizona. Hohokam Indian ruins on site. Believed to have been occupied 200 B.C. to 1400 A.D. on exact location. Outdoor Exhibit and Overlook illustrate ingenuity of early Arizona Indians. Inside are many fascinating art and craft exhibits. Hours: Monday to Friday 9 a.m. to 4:45 p.m.; also Sunday 1 p.m. to 4 p.m.

OTHER MUSEUMS NEAR PHOENIX

Mesa Museum

53 N. MacDonald Street, Mesa. Museum features clever exhibits for all ages. One can try his hand at panning for gold or learning to use ancient Hohokam tools. Hours: Tuesday- Saturday 10 a.m. to 4 p.m.

Salt River Project History Center

1521 Project Drive, Tempe. Photographs, prehistoric artifacts and films illustrate the past, present and future of the Salt River Valley and the Salt River Project.

Tempe Historical Museum

Southern & Rural in Tempe at the Tempe Community Center. Has everything from a Western chuckwagon to a Territorial post office; also farm implements, tools, toys and clothing from early days of Tempe. Hours: Tuesday-Saturday 9 a.m. to 5 p.m.

Buckeye

Buckeye Historical & Archeological Museum: 196 E. Highway 80. Exhibits include relics of prehistoric Indian civilizations. Many of the items are related to bygone pioneer life in the local area. Hours: Tuesday-Sunday 1 p.m. to 5 p.m. Closed Monday.

Florence

Pinal County Historical Society Museum: 5th & Main. This museum has many examples of Florence's frontier days on exhibit, Hours: Wednesday-Sunday 1 p.m. to 5 p.m.

Globe

City Hall: In town. Here one can study the artifacts found at the Salado pueblo called Besh-ba-Gowah. The actual pueblo is a mile south of town. Hours: open daily.

NORTH CENTRAL & NORTHERN ARIZONA

Flagstaff

The Museum of Northern Arizona: Two miles north of Flagstaff on Highway 180 (Fort Valley Road); only a five minute drive from the center of town. Exhibits of art, archeology, geology and natural history. In July, there is the traditional summer craftsmen's shows. However, the emphasis is on the art of the Navajo and the Hopi. Season is March-December. Hours vary, so inquire.

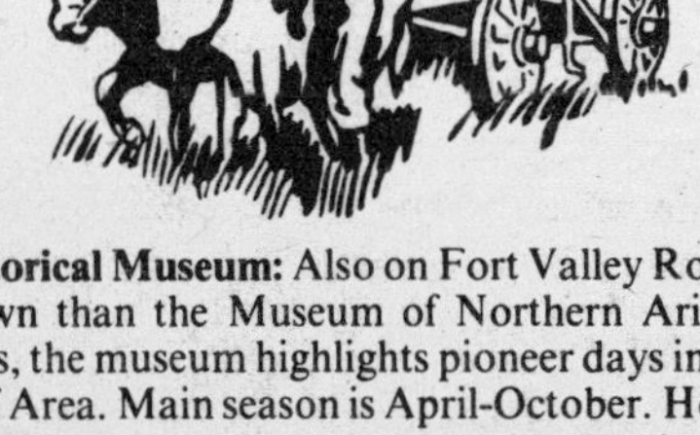

Pioneer Historical Museum: Also on Fort Valley Road, one mile closer to town than the Museum of Northern Arizona. As its name implies, the museum highlights pioneer days in and around the Flagstaff Area. Main season is April-October. Hours vary, so inquire.

Grand Canyon Village: Located in the Grand Canyon National Park. Exceptional and authentic exhibits at the Tustayan Museum, Visitor Center and Yavapai Museum. Check at Grand Canyon Village for the hours.

Prescott

Sharlot Hall Museum: 400 W. Gurley, in the Old Governor's Mansion at Pioneer Square. One of the best examples of Early Arizona art and artifacts; also some outstanding Indian relics and pioneer articles. Hours: 9 a.m. to noon and 1 p.m. to 5 p.m. Monday-Saturday; Sunday 1 p.m. to 5 p.m.

Smoki Museum: On Arizona Avenue, just North of E. Gurley Street. The Smoki people are a "tribe" of whites in Prescott, mainly business people, who organized in the 1920's and have painstakingly studied the Indian cultures of the southwest. Once a year they hold a Ceremonial Indian Dance in Prescott* highly regarded by the critics, before as many as 3,000 fans.

The museum itself has many fine examples of Indian masks, pottery and paintings. It also contains artifacts from Yavapai County Indian ruins. Main season: June through August. Hours: 10 a.m. to 4 p.m. weekdays; Sunday 1 p.m. to 4 p.m.

SOUTHERN ARIZONA

Tucson

Tucson is a city rich in tradition and the heritage of the Southwest. Her museums, most of which are FREE, are among the best the state has to offer.

Arizona Historical Society: 949 E. 2nd Street. The history of the state is presented in documents, photos and dioramas. They illustrate the Spanish, Mexican and American influences. Hours: 8 a.m. to 4 p.m. Monday-Friday; 8 a.m. to 1 p.m. on Saturday.

Arizona State Museum: On the campus of the University of Arizona. There is special emphasis on the prehistoric and modern cultures of Arizona's Indian tribes. Hours: 10 a.m. to 5 p.m. weekdays; 2 p.m. to 5 p.m. on Sundays.

***Admission is charged for the dance.**

Fort Lowell Museum: Craycroft Road and Fort Lowell Road. Good example of furnishings and articles that portray life on an early Arizona military post. The museum itself is a reconstructed Commanding Officer's Quarters. Hours: Tuesday-Saturday 10 a.m. to 4 p.m. Closed July-August.

Kitt Peak National Observatory: This world famous facility, the world's largest astronomical complex, is 56 miles southwest of Tucson via State Highway 86. It is 6,892 feet up in the Quinlan Mountains of the Sonoran Desert. The Visitor Center and the 4-meter telescopes are open to the public. Pick up free brochures for the famous walking tour. Visit the small museum. No food facilities, but has wooded picnic area. Hours: 10 a.m. to 4 p.m. daily except Christmas.

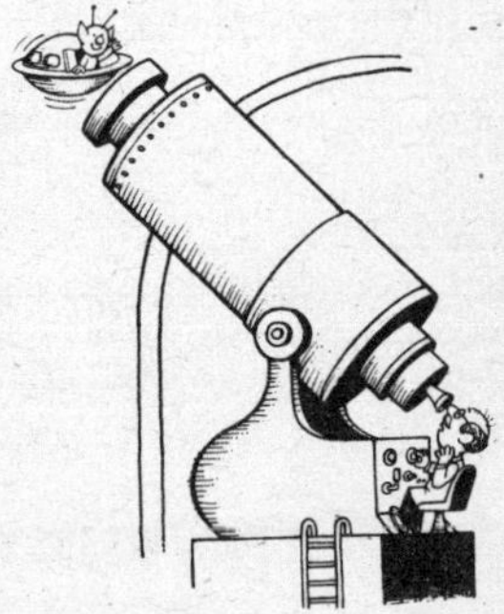

Mineralogical Museum: On the campus of the Univeristy of Arizona in Tucson. Has an outstanding selection of gemstones and fossils. The various displays illustrate the extraordinary variety of minerals found in the state. Hours: 8:30 a.m. to 4:30 p.m. Monday-Friday; 8 a.m. to noon on Saturday.

Tucson Museum of Art: 235 W. Alameda. The museum features changing exhibits in Fine Arts and Craft media. Permanent collections include Pre-Columbian, Spanish, Colonial, 20th Century European and American art. Hours: 10 a.m. to 5 p.m. Tuesday-Saturday; 1 p.m. to 5 p.m. on Sunday.

University of Arizona (Museum of Art): Located on the campus of the University. Important permanent collections span the periods from the Middle Ages through the 20th Century. Hours: 10 a.m. to 5 p.m. Tuesday-Friday; 1 p.m. to 5 p.m. on Sunday.

Bisbee

Bisbee Memorial Museum: In the Chamber of Commerce. This museum features mementos of this colorful historical mining town. Hours: Open 9 a.m. to 5 p.m. weekdays.

Restoration Museum: In the Fair Store Building at 37 Main Street. Four floors of displays recapturing Bisbee's history. Articles range from a blackjack table to antique style furniture and head-to-toe clothing from early pioneer days. There are literally thousands of items on display. Check with the Bisbee Chamber of Commerce for season and hours.

Dragoon

Amerind Foundation Inc. Museum: Off State Highway 86, and east of Benson. The museum has one of the most comprehensive collections of Indian and Mexican relics in the country. Open by appointment on Saturdays and Sundays.

Fort Huachuca

Fort Huachuca Historical Museum: Building 41401 on the Fort. The museum artifacts tell the story of the Fort's history and how the Apache Tribe conducted warfare. Hours: open Monday-Friday 9 a.m. to 4 p.m.; Sunday 1 p.m. to 4 p.m.

OTHER AREAS OF THE STATE

Kingman

Museum in Mohave Chamber of Commerce: On US 66 in downtown Kingman. Exhibits are devoted to life in the surrounding territory of Kingman. Hours: open daily 9 a.m. to 5 p.m.

Yuma

Century House: 248 Madison Avenue. Has exhibits, collections and Territorial Rooms in the style of particular period in Yuma history. Also has art gallery and literature section. Open October-June. Check with the Yuma Chamber of Commerce for current hours.

Yuma Territorial Prison Museum: At the Prison Site. This is a unique kind of museum with remains of a large cell block. Exhibits here reflect the prison life of inmates. Visitors can also tour dungeon and prison graveyard.

CHAPTER 7

MINES

Arizona history and mining are synonymous. The quest for mineral wealth was even pursued by Indians who experts believe mined turquoise as early as 1200 A.D.

There are many Arizona mining tales filled with color and romance . . . stories about hard-boiled prospectors, mountain-men, soldiers and pioneers. Over 400,000 mining claims have been recorded in the Grand Canyon State since its inception as a Territory. According to the records, some 4,000 companies were formed for the purpose of mining.

At first miners came to Arizona looking for gold and silver. They also found copper. However, it wasn't until 1879 that copper became vitally important to the outside world. That was the year Edison perfected the light bulb. Cities like New York and London required miles of copper wire for their electric generators. Transmission lines called for even more copper and Arizona had it!

At this time, Arizona copper ore was hauled by burro to the Colorado River. There, the ore was transported by boat to the Gulf of California where it was loaded on sea-going vessels which went "round the horn" to Swansea, Wales (England) where it was processed.

Today, Arizona produces more copper than all the other states combined. The dollar volume from copper mining is among the top three revenue producers in the state.

MID-CENTRAL
(Miami, Globe, Hayden Areas)

Hayden

Kennecott Minerals Company
Ray Mines Division: Open pit mine at Hayden. Public tours are given the last Thursday of each month. Call 356-7811, extension 378 for reservations. The meeting point is at the Administration Building at Hayden, 10 a.m. Group tours require at least two months notice.

Inspiration
Inspiration Consolidated Copper Company: Public tours available from Monday to Friday, usually from June to August at 9 a.m.; September to May at 12:45 p.m. Make reservations in advance for all tours. Call 473-2411, The Rock Shop.

Miami Area

Cities Service Company
Pinto Valley Mine: Open pit, west of Miami. No regular tour program available, but it is possible to arrange for special tours in advance. Write to Public Relations Dept., Cities Service Company, P.O. Box 100, Miami, AZ 85539.

Ranchers Exploration & Development Corporation:
Bluebird Mine: Open Pit, west of Miami. Special group tours are accepted by advanced reservation. Call 473-4405.

Casa Grande Area

Asarco, Incorporated
Sacaton Unit: Open pit north of Casa Grande. Contact the Manager at 882-0930 for group tours.

Prescott Area

McAlester Fuel Company
Zonia Mine: In-place leaching at Kirkland, southwest of Prescott. No tours available.

NORTHEASTERN ARIZONA

Bagdad

Cyrus Bagdad Copper Company
Bagdad Mine: Open pit mine. Public tours are given at 2 p.m., Saturday only. Departure is from the Shopping Center. Reservations must be made in advance. Call 633-2241.

Kingman area

Duval Corporation
Mineral Park Mine: Open pit, north of Kingman. Group tours only — and by advanced reservation. Call 565-2226.

SOUTHERN & SOUTHEASTERN ARIZONA

Ajo

Phelps Dodge Corporation
New Cornelia Mine: Open pit at Ajo. Overlook available. Special tours by advanced reservation. Public tours must be prearranged. Call Employment Office at 387-7611 to make reservations.

Douglas

Phelps Dodge Corporation
Tours of smelter conducted on Tuesday of each week, beginning at 1 p.m. Contact Smelter Superintendent on weekdays from 7 a.m. to 4 p.m. at 364-2441, or write: P.O. Drawer E, Douglas, AZ 85607.

Johnson

Cyrus Johnson Copper Company
Open pit mine. Group tours are accepted, but by reservation only. Call 884-8362.

Morenci

Phelps Dodge Corporation
Open pit and smelter. Tours of concentrator are offered five days a week, beginning at 9:30 a.m. Contact the Manager at 865-3772 for reservations. However, the Public Viewpoint is open 24 hours a day, 7 days a week with a recorded message.

Near Tucson

Anamax Mining Company
Open pit mines south of Tucson. Overlook open from dawn to dusk. Take I-19 at Duval Mine Road, proceed ¾ mile west. Follow signs from there. Public tours are given at 9 a.m. on Tuesday and Thursday, by reservation. For group tours, call 884-7845, Extension 201.

Asarco Incorporated
Mission Unit: Open pit mine south of Tucson. Call Manager at 622-4891 to arrange group tours.

Silver Bell Unit: Open pit mine northwest of Tucson. Call Manager at 622-6751 to arrange group tours.

Because of the distances from major cities, we suggest contacting the individual mines before setting out on a trip. For special up-to-the-minute information on mines, write to: Arizona Mining Association, 100 West Clarendon, Suite 1720, Phoenix, Arizona 85013.

CHAPTER 8

NATIONAL FORESTS, CAMPING & CAMPGROUNDS

NATIONAL FORESTS

There are seven National Forests in Arizona, covering more than 11 million acres of the state's greenest and most gorgeous scenery. All include a variety of camping sites and picnic areas. Many also contain excellent boating, swimming, hunting and fishing facilities. Following is a short synopsis of each forest with a list of the major facilities and attractions:

Apache National Forest: Consists of approximately 1,808,000 acres, some of which are in New Mexico. Forest headquarters is in Springerville in eastern Arizona. The area has numerous scenic drives through one of the largest stands of Ponderosa Pine in the Southwest. Lakes, streams and meadows support a variety of wildlife, including elk, deer, antelope and turkey. The renowned Coronado Trail through Alpine and across the Mogollon Rim is an especially beautiful drive.

There are 27 Forest Service camping and picnic sites in the Apache National Forest, and fishing is good in the various lakes and streams. Horseback riding and boating are among the other recreational opportunities available. Apache National Forest ranges in elevation from 5,000 to 11,500 feet. Accommodations are available in Alpine, Greer and Springerville.

Coconino National Forest: Consists of approximately 1,999,000 acres in northern Arizona with headquarters in Flagstaff. The forest area is composed largely of rolling terrain. The southern portion is cut by deep gorges and canyons. In the north the San Francisco peaks rise to 12,680 feet—the highest point in Arizona. Outstanding scenic features are Oak Creek Canyon and the Mogollon Rim. The *Arizona Snow Bowl Winter Sports Area* is also within the forest. National Monuments within or near the forest include Wupatki, Sunset Crater and Walnut Canyon.

The Forest Service operates 23 camping and picnic sites in Coconino, and trout fishing is rated as especially good. Boating is enjoyed on lakes Mary, Ashurst, Kinnikinick and Blue Ridge. Horseback riding is readily available, along with all types of winter sports at the Snow Bowl. Coconino National Forest ranges in elevation from 3,500 feet to 12,500 feet. Accommodations are available in Flagstaff, Clarkdale, Sedona and Winslow.

Coronado National Forest: Covers 1,8000,000 acres divided up into 12 scattered, non-adjacent sections, part of which are in New Mexico. Forest headquarters is at Tucson in southeastern Arizona. The terrain varies from arid desert to rugged, wooded mountains, with snow skiing and swimming only 40 miles apart. Scenic drives include Hitchcock Highway to Mount Lemmon ski area, Mount Graham Road, Ruby Road, Onion Saddle Road, US 80, and Rucker Canyon Road.

Saguaro and Chiricahua National Monuments, Coronado National Memorial, and Cochise Stronghold are all within the Coronado National Forest.

The Forest Service maintains 49 camping and picnic sites in the Coronado preserve. Fishing, paok trips, hiking trails and boating can all be enjoyed. Coronado National Forest ranges in elevation from 4,000 to 11,000 feet. Accommodations are available at Tucson, Nogales, Safford, Tombstone, Willcox and Douglas.

Kaibab National Forest: Covers 1,725,000 acres in four scattered divisions with headquarters at Williams in north-central Arizona. The forest lies both north and south of the Grand Canyon, and includes access routes to the Havasupai Indian Village and to both rims of the Grand Canyon. Recreational facilities are extensive in the Grand Canyon National Park (see listing). Fishing and swimming are popular at Whitehorse Lake. Kaibab National Forest ranges in elevation from 5,000 to 7,000 feet. Accomodations are available at Williams, Grand Canyon and Fredonia.

Prescott National Forest: Consists of approximatley 1,250,000 acres in central Arizona with headquarters at Prescott. The forest covers two long mountain ranges which vary in elevation from 3,000 to 8,000 feet. Besides the major access routes of US 89, 89A and I-17, there are numerous scenic, but unimproved roads winding through the backwoods. Major points of interest are the Tuzigoot and Montezuma Castle National Monuments.

The Forest Service maintains 16 camping and picnic sites. Bathing and fishing are favorite activities at Granite Basin and Horse Thief Basin. The Lynx Lake Recreation Area, just east of Prescott, and the Mingus Mountain Recreation Area, just south of Jerome are also in the vicinity. Accommodations are available at Prescott, Cottonwood, Camp Verde and Sedona.

Sitgreaves National Forest: Consisting of approximately 808,000 acres, this is the smallest national forest in the southwest. The forest is situated on the south edge of the Colorado Plateau in central Arizona with headquarters at Holbrook. The area provides livestock grazing, wildlife habitat and extensive outdoor recreation. Near Snowflake the only pulp and paper mill in the southwest produces more than 400 tons of paper every day.

Four developed camping and picnic sites are maintained by the Forest Service. Fine trout fishing is available in the eight cold water lakes, and numerous mountain streams. Boating is popular, and at Lakeside, Woods Canyon Lake and Canyon Point guided nature walks are conducted regularly. Sitgreaves National Forest varies in elevation from 5,000 to 8,000 feet. Accommodations are available at Holbrook, Show Low and Payson.

Tonto National Forest: Covers 2,960,000 acres in east central Arizona with headquarters in Phoenix. About one-quarter of the forest is inaccessible because of wilderness, mountains and lack of adequate roads. The landscape varies tremendously, from arid cactus-laden desert in the south to lush pine forests in the north. Scenic drives are plentiful and popular, and include the renowned Apache Trail, Beeline Highway and Payson-Mogollon Rim Roads.

Six large man-made lakes (Roosevelt, Apache, Canyon, Saguaro, Bartlett and Horseshoe) cover 16,000 acres and provide the nearby metropolitan population with an abundance of water-centered recreational opportunities. Fishing, boating, bathing and water-skiing are among the favorite activities. Bass and trout are the predominant fish.

The Forest Service maintains 28 camping and picnic sites inside the Tonto Forest. Tonto National Forest varies in elevation from 4,000 to 7,900 feet. Accommodations are available at Tempe, Mesa, Apache Junction, Globe and Miami.

NATIONAL RECREATION AREAS

Glen Canyon National Recreation Area

Just north of Page on the Arizona-Utah border, this area was created when the Glen Canyon Dam was completed in 1963. The dam-formed Lake Powell—186 miles long—boasts some of the finest facilities in the state for fishing, boating and water sports. The spot is one of the fastest growing recreational areas in the United States.

Carl Hayden Visitor Center: This multi-million dollar facility overlooks the dam and much of scenic Lake Powell. Numerous colorful displays illustrate the construction of the dam and explain the area's geology and history. A self-guided tour through the dam begins and ends at the Center. The visitor Center is open 7 a.m. to 7 p.m. daily in the summer; 8:30 a.m. to 5 p.m. the rest of the year.

Lake Powell: This man-made water playground stretches 186 miles up the Colorado River, well into southern Utah. The lake has almost 2,000 miles of shoreline when filled to capacity, and provides an ever-changing array of scenery stretching into hidden canyons, coves and inlets, and winding its way through mountainous red sand dunes carved by ancient seas, winds and erosion.

Vistors have a wide range of recreational opportunities to selct from. Swimming along sandy beaches is always a favorite diversion. The more adventurous can water-ski through channels and bays. Boats of all types go exploring well away from the main hub of activity. Fishing for trout, bass or catfish is also an ever-popular sport. A valid state license is required and is available at the Visitor Center, as is a copy of state fishing regulations. Lake facilities include:

Bullfrog Marina. Just off Highway 95 at Trachyte, Utah, this site offers camping, swimming, picnicking, rental boats of all sizes and varieties, and a trailer village. **Halls Crossing.** Ninety-five miles west of Blanding, Utah, this site includes a campground, boat rentals, marina and trailer village.

Hite Marina. Fifty miles southeast of Hanksville, Utah, this area includes facilities for swimming, fishing and camping. **Lee's Ferry.** Five miles from Marble Canyon and about 50 miles south of the dam, Lee's Ferry is a major recreational site, with boat rentals and a campground. Colorado River excursions depart from here. **Wahweap.** Nine miles west of Page, Wahweap is National Park Service headquarters for Glen Canyon and one of the primary recreational spots at Lake Powell. A marina with rental boats, campground, picnic sites, swimming beach and trailer village are among the facilities.

Other facilities are being built and local inquiry at the Visitor Center is advised regarding the most recent recreational developments. Also see listings under boating, camping, lakes, etc.

Lake Mead National Recreation Area

In the northwest corner of the state, Lake Mead, formed by Hoover Dam and extending up into Nevada, was long regarded as Arizona's premier recreational region. Lake Mead Recreation Area extends some 240 miles along the Colorado River and is a multi-state haven for boating, fishing, swimming and a variety of water sports.

Hoover Dam: Completed in 1935, the dam is the largest of all federal reclamation projects and the highest dam in the Western Hemisphere—726 feet. At the top, Hoover Dam is 1,244 feet long and 45 feet thick. At the bottom, the structure is 660 feet thick. Visitors can take guided tours through the dam.
Visitor Center: Four miles from Boulder City, Nevada at Boulder Beach, the Center features an exhibit building with a topographical model of the dam and surroundig area, a 12 minute free movie, and information services. Besides the Visitor Center, Boulder Beach has a modern lodge complete with swimming pool, marina and bathouse. Park rangers conduct illustrated evening talks at the amphitheaters in Boulder Beach, Katherine and Temple Bar during the spring, summer and fall.

Lake Mead: One of the largest artificial lakes in the world, Lake Mead holds nearly 30 million acre-feet of water, is 115 miles long, contains some 550 miles of shoreline, and reaches a depth of 589 feet. Looking out upon the lake, one sees some of the bluest, loveliest water-desert panoramas in the Southwest.

Around the lake are six individual recreation centers. The only one in Arizona is Temple Bar, about 80 miles north of Kingman. In Nevada are Boulder Beach, six miles northeast of Boulder City; Callville Bay, 16 miles northwest of Las Vegas Wash; Las Vegas Wash, seven miles northeast of Boulder Beach; and the Overton Landing and Echo Bay areas, 15 miles south of Glendale.

Launching ramps, campgrounds, boat rentals and refreshment concessions are available at most of these sites. All except Las Vegas Wash and Callville Bay offer overnight accommodations. A Visitor Center is located at Boulder Beach. One-hour boat excursions leave several times daily from the Lake Mead Marina, northeast of Boulder City. The trip passes near the colorful Paint Pots and Fortification Hill on the way to Black Canyon and Hoover Dam.

Ferry Boat service is available between Boulder Beach and Callville and Echo Bays. Trips leave daily at 10 a.m. from the Lake Mead Marina and at 1 p.m. from Echo Bay.

Lake Mohave: Some 68 miles south of Hoover Dam, Lake Mohave behind Davis Dam boasts four other recreational developments. These include *Katherine,* about 35 miles west of Kingman on Highway 68 near Davis Dam; and *Willow Beach,* about 65 miles northwest of Kingman off US 93-466. *Eldorado Canyon,* 37 miles south of Boulder City; and *Cottonwood Cove* 15 miles east of Searchlight, are in Nevada.

Launching ramps, trailer sites, refreshment concessions, boat rentals and overnight accommodations are available at each of these four areas. Only Katherine has swimming facilities. Campsites are maintained at all but Eldorado Canyon. Information stations are set up at Willow Beach, Cottonwood Cove and Katherine.

Picnic facilities are scattered throughout the entire recreational area. Cabin facilities are available at many of the beaches. Motel accommodations are available in Katherine, Kingman and Boulder City, Nevada. The Lake Mead National Recreation Area covers almost two million acres and provides fun-seekers with a wide range of enjoyable and relaxing recreational facilities.

See other listings under boating, camping, lakes, fishing, etc. for additional information.

Picnicking—In Arizona, picnicking can be enjoyed the yearround and is rarely hampered by long drenching rains or bitter cold weather. For some, a picnic means a lunch-time stop at a roadside rest area for sandwiches and cool (or hot!) drinks. For others, it means a Sunday outing at a city park with family and friends; a summertime trek up to the cool mountain country; or maybe a jaunt into the desert in search of a private, peaceful place in the sun (or shade).

Whatever your fancy, picnicking is fun and popular and developed picnic sites are plentiful. For a listing of facilities, see the charts in the "Camping" section.

Hiking—This is another very popular form of exercise and recreation for Arizona residents and visitors. National Forests and Monuments are favorite locales for hikers and mountain climbers.

The Grand Canyon has many hiking trails for the rugged adventurist as well as the casual walker. Arizona's forests are loaded with hiking possibilities. Desert hiking is also popular but can be extremely strenuous and dangerous in hot weather without adequate preparation. Almost any area in the state lends itself to hiking, but caution is advised for those planning extended hikes. Desert heat, dust storms, flash floods, blizzards and extremely low temperatures are among the potential hazards, depending on the area and the season.

There are numerous hiking paths and nature trails within state, county, and municipal parks. Encanto Park in Phoenix, for instance, has an extremely interesting self-guided nature walk. A brochure guide is available from the recreation Branch Office at 2700 N. 15th Avenue, Phoenix 85007. Specific information about local hiking conditions can be obtained from officials at the various parks, monuments and recreation areas. Also, local Chambers of Commerce can provide a list of hiking clubs in the area.

Nature Walks—Arizona abounds in natural beauty and contains many unusual and in some cases unique natural phenomena. A number of nature walks can be taken around the state—some guided and some self-guided—to accommodate those interested in examining a sampling of the more interesting treasures nature has provided.

Some of the most outstanding nature trails can be found at the following:

Coronado National Memorial, Montezuma Castle National Monument (Sycamore Trail), Chiricahua National Monument, Sunset Crater National Monument, Grand Canyon (north and south rims), Petrified Forest, Encanto Park tree walk (Phoenix), Mingus Mountain area, Palm Canyon and Kofa Game Range, Tonto National Monument, Arizona Sonora Deseert Museum, Mt. Lemmon, Sabino Canyon and Tucson Mountain Park.

Forest Fires

Forest fires are rather common in Arizona, many occurring as a result of natural causes, such as lightning or spontaneous combustion. Unfortunately, many also are started as a result of human carelessness. Usually, the greatest fire danger in the state occurs in late spring and early summer when it is very hot, and before the late summer thunderstorms relieve the parched land. Restrictions are frequently put into effect regarding campfires and travel into the forests. For information on current conditions, contact the National Forest Service in Phoenix at 230 N. 1st Avenue, or phone 261-3205. Signs are posted during restricted periods.

FISH HATCHERIES

To keep Arizona's rivers and lakes well-stocked for sportsmen, the state maintains several fish hatcheries that are open to the public. These include:

Alchesay National Fish Hatchery: Located 8 miles north of Whiteriver on Highway 73.

Page Springs Fish Hatchery: About 25 minutes southwest of Sedona at Cornville off US 89 alternate.

Silver Springs Fish Hatchery: About 20 minutes northeast of Show Low on Highway 61.

Sterling Springs Fish Hatchery: Located just above Page Springs.

Tonto Creek Hatchery: On highway 160 about 20 minutes east of Payson, near Kohl's Ranch.

Williams Creek Hatchery: Twenty minutes northeast of Whiteriver on Highway 73.

Willow Beach Hatchery: On US 93 about an hour northwest of Kingman.

CAMPING & CAMPGROUNDS

Arizona's weather, especially its dry climate, favors camping. Northern Arizona generally has cool, comfortable summers, and its winters although cold and snowy, are mostly free from extreme severity. The desert winters range from warm to cool during the day, and from cool to fairly cold at night.

This chapter deals only with campgrounds and areas under the jurisdiction of the U.S. Forest Service, U.S. National Park Service, Bureau of Land Management, Arizona State Parks and those operated by county and local governments. There are many more sites, commercial and Indian tribal, available throughout Arizona. Check the listings in the local telephone directories for their locations.

Arizona camping can be enjoyed in a variety of landscapes. There is truly something for everyone's taste and moods. For example, the camper can encounter a wide range of wildlife in the Grand Canyon State: mammals, birds, reptiles and insects. Most of them are harmless. However, always shake out bedding and shoes before use. Most people never see a rattlesnake or a Gila Monster (a small, lizard-like creature). But if you do, neither should ever be teased.

Be sure to find out if the area where you plan to camp out requires a free permit and/or reservation. Some areas do. Also, check with the Game and Fish Department for rules and regulations. Write Department of Game & Fish, 2222 West Greenway Road Phoenix, Arizona 85023. This is especially important if you plan to hunt while visiting. They will advise you on permits and licensing.

For the approximate location of the camping area you are planning to arrive at, check the small scale map on the opposite page for the correct area number. Some areas marked with the letter "P" indicate a primitive area. Please note: only *free* campgrounds have been listed here. For a complete guide to all the campsites, including those with fees, write to:
Arizona Office of Tourism
3507 N. Central Avenue
Phoenix, Arizona 85012

Camping Facts

The U.S. Forest Service and the Department of Agriculture provide on-going forest and campground information for Arizona residents and visitors. For the latest recorded readout, call *Forest Facts,* 244-9701.

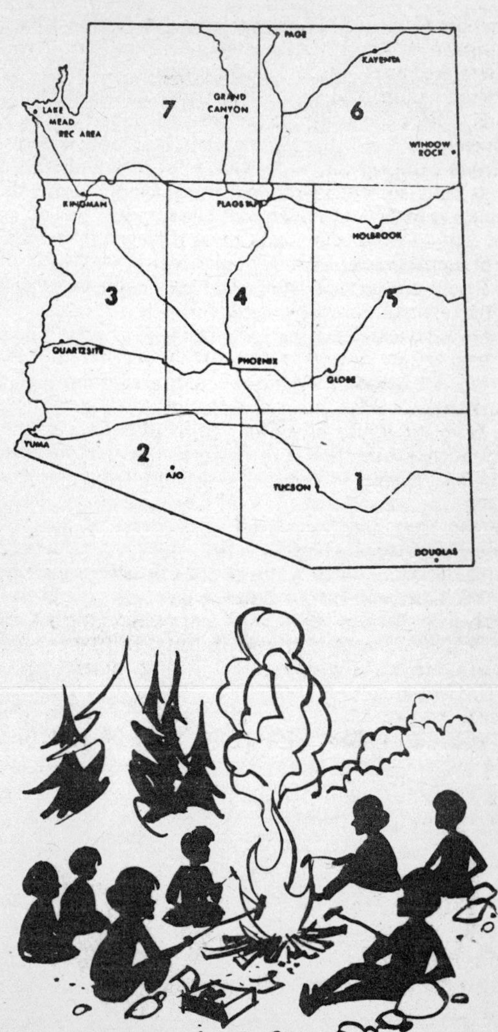
PAGE
KAYENTA
GRAND CANYON
7
6
LAKE MEAD REC AREA
WINDOW ROCK
KINGMAN
FLAGSTAFF
HOLBROOK
3
4
5
QUARTZSITE
PHOENIX
GLOBE
YUMA
2
AJO
TUCSON
1
DOUGLAS

GUIDELINES

The following guidelines and regulations for using parks and recreation areas was supplied by the Arizona Office of Tourism.

1. Avoid activities that result in the disturbance of ecological relationships.
2. Keep campfires small and always under control; completely quench when they are abandoned.
3. Leave the recreation site cleaner than you found it. Carry out all wastes created by your visit.
4. Check the availability of potable drinking water or carry enough water for your needs.
5. Do not camp near watering facilities used by wildlife or livestock.
6. Do not camp in washes or other areas with high flood potential.
7. Keep all vehicles on authorized roads and trails.
8. Do not disturb Indian artifacts, pictographs, petroglyphs, ruins, or other evidence of early cultures.
9. Do not collect petrified wood, fossils, gemstones and rocks from any park, recreation site, forest or campground unless otherwise posted.
10. Do not remove or damage cacti or other native plants. They are protected by Arizona law.
11. Observe all laws, including firearms and property laws.
12. Respect public and private property. Don't damage buildings, fences, sign gates, water developments, or picnic facilities.
13. Observe all state game and fish laws.
14. Pets are allowed out-of-doors, but must be kept under control at all times.
15. Regulations may vary according to season; check all regulations at the entrance of the area.

AREA 1

Symbols Used in the Listings: **B**-Boating **F**-Fishing **R**-Restrooms **RV**-Recreational Vehicle Facilities **T**-Tents **W**-Safe Water

Name of Site	General Location	Elevation	Season	Facilities
Aravaipa Canyon, East (p)	60 miles W of Safford (partly gravel)	3,000′	All Year	R, T
Round Mountain	10 miles S of Duncan	4,100′	All Year	T
Joy Valley	16 miles NE of Bowie	3,650′	All Year	RV, T
West Turkey Creek	36 miles NE of Elfrida	5,900′	February-November	R, RV, T
Sycamore Forest	38 miles NE of Elfrida	6,200′	February-November	R, RV, T
Pinery Canyon	15 miles W of Portal	7,000′	April-November	R, RV, T, W
John Hands	7 miles SW of Portal	5,600′	April-November	F, R, RV, T
Herb Matyr	8 miles SW of Portal	5,800′	April-November	F, R, RV, T, W
South Fork Forest	5 miles SW of Portal	5,300′	March-November	R, RV, T
Bear Canyon	27 miles NE of Tucson	5,800	All Year	W
Calabasas	13 miles NW of Nogales	4,000′	All Year	B, F, RV, T
Peppersauce	15 miles SE of Oracle	4,700′	All Year	R, RV, T, W
Aravaipa Canyon, West (p)	10 miles S of Winkleman (part gravel)	2,600′	All Year	R,T
Black Hills	17 miles S of Safford	4,000′	All Year	——
Safford-Morenci Trail/West	12 miles NE of Safford	4,700′	All Year	T
Four Mile Canyon	SW on Klondyke	3,500′	All Year	R, RV, T, W

AREA 2

Symbols Used in the Listings: **B**-Boating **F**-Fishing **R**-Restrooms **RV**-Recreational Vehicle Facilities **T**-Tents **W**-Safe Water

Name of Site	General Location	Elevation	Season	Facilities
Senator Wash	6 miles N of Laguna Dam	260′	All Year	B, F, R, RV, T

AREA 3

Name of Site	General Location	Elevation	Season	Facilities
Wild Cow Springs	5 miles past Hualapai Mountain Park	6,600′	May-October	R, RV, T
Burro Creek	55 miles N of Wickenburg	1,950′	All Year	R, RV, T, W
La Posa Recreation Area	¼ to 3 miles S of Quartzsite	875′	All Year	R, RV, T,
Crystal Hill	15 miles S of Quartzsite	1,480′	All Year	R, RV, T
Bullhead Community Park	¼ mile S of Bullhead City	675′	All Year	B, F, R, RV
Takeoff Point Recreation Site	AZ 95. 16 miles N of Parker, (W on dirt road)	450′	All Year	B, F

AREA 4

Name of Site	General Location	Elevation	Season	Facilities
Hazlett Hollow	10 miles SE of Crown King	6,000′	May-November	R, T, W
Turney Gulch	10 miles SE of Crown King	6,000′	May-November	F, R, T, W
Kentuck Springs	11 miles SE of Crown King	6,000′	April-November	R, RV, T, W
Cave Creek	21 miles NE of Carefree	3,500′	All Year	RV, T
Seven Springs	20 miles NE of Carefree	3,400′	All Year	RV, T

AREA 4 (Continued)

Symbols Used in the Listings: **B**-Boating **F**-Fishing **R**-Restrooms **RV**-Recreational Vehicle Facilities **T**-Tents **W**-Safe Water

Horsehoe	23 miles NE of Carefree	1,900′	All Year	B, F, T
Bartlett Lake	20 miles E of Carefree	1,800′	All Year	B, F, RV, T
Horse Pasture	11 miles NW of Roosevelt Lake	2,100′	May-October	B, F, RV, T
Granite Reef	14 miles NE of Mesa	1,300′	All Year	F, RV, T
Ponderosa Group Camp	15 miles NE of Payson	5,600′	All Year	RV, T, W
Tonto Creek	17 miles NE of Payson	5,600′	May-September	F, T
Coon's Bluff	20 miles NE of Mesa	1,400′	All Year	F, RV, T
Bagley Flat	32 miles NE of Mesa	1,500′	All Year	B, F, T
Apache Lake Marina	33 miles NE of Apache Junction	1,900′	All Year	B, F, RV, T, W
The Point, Canyon Lake	19 miles NE of Apache Junction	1,700′	All Year	B, F, T
Burnt Corral	6 miles SW of Roosevelt Lake	1,800′	All Year	B, F, TV, T
Porter Springs	6 miles E of Roosevelt Lake	2,100′	All Year	B, F, RV, T
Windy Hill	6 miles E of Roosevelt Lake	2,100′	All Year	B, F, TV, T
Oak Flat	4 miles E of Superior	4,200′	All Year	R, RV, T
Sycamore	6 miles N of Payson	4,500′	All Year	——
Cataract Lake	1 mile W of Williams	6,800′	May-October	B, F, RV, T
Bootlegger	9 miles N of Sedona	4,400′	May-October	B, F, RV, T
Ashurst	20 miles SE of Flagstaff	7,000′	April-November	B, F, R, RV, T
Forked Pine	22 miles SE of Flagstaff	7,100′	April-November	B, F, R, RV, T, W

AREA 4 (Continued)

Symbols Used in the Listings: **B**-Boating **F**-Fishing **R**-Restrooms **RV**-Recreational Vehicle Facilities **T**-Tents **W**-Safe Water

Name of Site	General Location	Elevation	Season	Facilities
Red Rock	7 miles SW of Sedona	4,000′	All Year	F, R, RV, W
Hilltop	9 miles SW of Prescott	6,000′	April-November	F, RV
Potatoe Patch	7 miles SW of Jerome	6,500′	May-November	R, RV, T
Mingus Mountain	9 miles SW of Jerome	7,600′	April-November	R, RV, T
Powell Springs	13 miles NE of Dewey	5,300′	All Year	R, RV, T, W
Indian Creek	4 miles SW of Prescott	5,800′	May-October	R, RV, T
Kinnikinick Lake	33 miles SE of Flagstaff	7,000′	May-October	B, F, R, RV, T
Clint's Well Campgrounds	15 miles S of Happy Jack	7,000′	May-November	R, RV, T, W
Kehl Springs	26 miles S of Happy Jack	7,500′	May-November	R, RV, T, W
Lakeview	16 miles SE of Flagstaff	6,900′	April-October	B, F, R, T, W
Riverside	23 miles E of Carefree	1,600′	All Year	T
Orange Peel Pt.	12 miles NW of Roosevelt Lake	2,100′	All Year	B, F, RV, T
Angler's Inn	11 miles NW of Roosevelt Lake	2,100′	All Year	B, F, RV, T
Cholla Bay	10 miles NW of Roosevelt Lake	2,200′	All Year	B, F, RV, T
Bachelor's Cove	9 miles NW of Roosevelt Lake	2,200′	All Year	B, F, RV, T
Hotel Point	2½ miles NW of Roosevelt Lake	2,100′	All Year	F, T
Roosevelt Marina	½ mile NW of Roosevelt Lake	2,100′	All Year	B, F, RV, T

AREA 4 (Continued)

Symbols Used in the Listings: **B**-Boating **F**-Fishing **R**-Restrooms **RV**-Recreational Vehicle Facilities **T**-Tents **W**-Safe Water

Name of Site	General Location	Elevation	Season	Facilities
School House Point	1 mile E of Roosevelt Lake	2,100′	All Year	B, F, RV, T
Cottonwoods	22 miles E of Roosevelt	2,200′	All Year	F, RV, T
Diversion Dam	19 miles E of Roosevelt Lake	2,200′	All Year	F, RV, T
Lakeview Trailer Park	At Roosevelt Lake	2,100′	All Year	B, F, RV, T, W

AREA 5

Name of Site	General Location	Elevation	Season	Facilities
White Mountain Lake	4 miles NW of Silver Creek	6,200′	All Year	B, F, RV
Rose Creek	23 miles S of Young	5,400′	May-November	R, RV, T, W
Jones Water	17 miles NE of Globe	4,500′	All Year	R, RV, T, W
Pinal Mountain	15 miles SW of Globe	7,500′	May-October	R, T, W
Pioneer Pass	9 miles S of Globe	6,000′	April-December	R, RV, T, W
Chevelon Lake	44 miles SW of Winslow	6,400′	April-October	B, RV, T
Chevelon Canyon Lake	18 miles NW of Heber	6,200′	All Year	F, T
Canyon Creek	31 miles NE of Young	6,700′	May-October	F, RV, T
Gentry	18 miles SW of Heber	7,700′	April-October	R, RV, T
Fool Hollow	6 miles NW of Show Low	6,300′	May-November	B, F, R, RV, T

AREA 5 (Continued)

Symbols Used in the Listings: **B**-Boating **F**-Fishing **R**-Restrooms **RV**-Recreational Vehicle Facilities **T**-Tents **W**-Safe Water

Name of Site	General Location	Elevation	Season	Facilities
South Fork Camp	5 miles W of Springerville	7,700′	June-September	RV, T
Diamond Rock	10 miles SW of Alpine	7,900′	May-October	F, RV, T
Aspen	10 miles W of Alpine	7,500′	May-October	F, RV, T
Stray Horse	26 miles S of Alpine on US 666	8,200′	May-October	R, RV, T, W
K.P. Cienega	23 miles SW of Alpine	9,000′	June-September	RV, T
Hannagan Meadow	18 miles SW of Alpine	9,100′	June-September	RV, T
Upper Blue Springs	6 miles N of Blue	6,200′	May-December	F, RV, T
Blue Crossing	2 miles N of Blue	6,200′	May December	RV, T
Juan Miller Upper	26 miles NW of Clifton	6,100′	May-October	T
Juan Miller Lower	27 miles NW of Clifton	6,000′	May-October	RV, T
Granville	16 miles NW of Clifton	5,000′	April-October	T, W
Grey's Peak	22 miles NW of Clifton	6,000′	May-October	RV, T, W
Sheep Crossing	6 miles SW of Greer	8,700′	June-September	F
Valentine Ridge	28 miles NE of Young	6,500′	May-October	RV, T
Safford-Morenci Trail	6 miles SE of Morenci	6,000′	All Year	T
Benny Creek	2 miles N of Greer	8,500′	May-September	B, F
Lewis Canyon	2 miles S of Pineville	6,500′	May-October	RV, T

AREA 6

Symbols Used in the Listings: **B**-Boating **F**-Fishing **R**-Restrooms **RV**-Recreational Vehicle Facilities **T**-Tents **W**-Safe Water

Name of Site	General Location	Elevation	Season	Facilities
Wahweap	7 miles NW of Page	3,800′	All Year	B, F, R, RV, T, W
Cottonwood	Canyon de Chelly National Park	5,500′	All Year	R, RV, T, W

AREA 7

Name of Site	General Location	Elevation	Season	Facilities
Windy Point	21 miles US 93, N of Kingman	6,200′	May-October	R, RV, T
Cottonwood, Inner Canyon	N. Kaibab Trail	4,200′	April-October	R, T, W
Phantom Ranch, Inner Canyon	———	2,450′	All Year	R, T, W
Roaring Springs, Inner Canyon	N. Kaibab Trail	5,200′	April-October	T
Boneli Landing	75 miles NW of Kingman	1,230′	All Year	B, F, RV, T
Toro Weap Point	72 miles SW of Fredonia	5,600′	All Year	R, RV, T
Gregg's Hideout	70 miles N of Kingman	1,288′	All Year	B, F, RV, T
Indian Gardens, Grand Canyon	Bright Angel Trail	3,800′	All Year	R, T, W

CHAPTER 9

BOATING & FISHING

Arizona is often mistakenly thought of as all desert; yet boating is one of the biggest sporting activities on its many fine lakes. Arizona ranks high as to the number of boats in relation to it's population. On any given summer weekend boating enthusiasts jam highways leading towards the lake country.

Fishing on Arizona lakes is also a major recreation. Be sure to obtain a license, either from any Arizona Game & Fish Department office, or a conveniently located Yellow Front store in the sporting goods department. Fees vary as to residents and non-residents; also there are extra stamps (fees) issued for certain kinds of fish and certain lakes.

BOATING REQUIREMENTS

Before taking a boat out on the lake in Arizona, there are certain basic items required to be on board:

1. **Fire extinguisher:** It's a state law. A Coast Guard approved fire extinguisher must be aboard any watercraft carrying gasoline.

2. **Flame Arrestors:** All inboard gasoline engines must be equipped with a backfire flame arrestor securely attached to each carburetor air intake.

3. **Ventilation:** Ventilation is required on all boats which use gasoline as a fuel and have an enclosed engine or fuel storage compartments.

4. **Lights:** Boats operating from sunset to sunrise are required to display navagational lights.

5. **Water Skiing:** In Arizona, water skiing is restricted to daylight hours. The towing boat must carry at least two people: an operator and an observer.
The operator must devote his full attention to the safe operation of the watercraft and observe other boats and swimmers. Care must be taken that the person being towed does not come too close to other boats, swimmers and structures.

For complete information on the subject of safety and regulations, send for *Arizona Boating Guide.* It is a handy, well-written 36-page booklet on all the things you need to know on the subject. Write to: Arizona Game & Fish Department, 2222 W. Greenway Road, Phoenix, AZ 85023. There is no charge.

Following is a list of Arizona's boating lakes; where they are located, and the kinds of fish available in their waters.

CENTRAL & NORTHERN ARIZONA

Name of Lake	Location	Elevation	Kinds of Fish
Apache Lake	32 miles NE of Apache Junction (some unpaved road)	1,914′	bass, catfish, crappie, panfish, walleye
Amhurst Lake	21 miles SE of Flagstaff	7,180′	trout
Barlett Lake	48 miles NE of Phoenix	1,798′	bass, catfish, crappie, panfish
Bear Canyon Lake	45 miles NE of Payson (some unpaved road)	7,500′	——
Black Canyon Lake	19 miles SW of Heber (some unpaved road)	7,000′	rainbow trout
Blue Ridge Reservoir	49 miles N of Payson (some unpaved road)	6,200′	trout
Canyon Lake	13 miles NE of Apache Junction	1,660′	bass, bluegill, catfish, crappie
Cataract Lake	2 miles W of Williams	6,800′	rainbow trout
Chevelon Canyon Lake	30 miles NE of Weber (some unpaved road)	6,000′	trout
Kaibab Lake	4 miles NE of Williams	6,800′	rainbow trout
Kinnikinick Lake	34 miles SE of Flagstaff	7,000′	trout
Knoll Lake	55 miles NE of Payson (some unpaved road)	7,500′	rainbow trout
Long Lake	44 miles NE of Pine	6,700′	bluegill, some bass, catfish, pike, some trout
Lynx Lake	8 miles SE of Prescott	6,000′	rainbow trout
Lake Mary	23 miles S of Flagstaff	6,900′	channel catfish, northern pike, some trout, walleye

CENTRAL & NORTHERN ARIZONA (Continued)

Name of Lake	Location	Elevation	Kinds of Fish
Lake Pleasant	30 miles NW of Phoenix	1,600′	bass, bluegill, channel catfish, crappie
Lake Powell	1 mile N of Page	3,700′	bass, bluegill, channel catfish, crappie, trout, walleye
Roosevelt Lake	30 miles NW of Phoenix	2,136′	bass, channel catfish, crappie, panfish
San Carlos Lake	20 miles SE of Globe	2,600′	bass, bluegill, channel catfish, crappie
Saguaro Lake	29 miles NE of Phoenix	1,529′	bass, bluegill, channel catfish, crappie, green sunfish
Willow Springs	32 miles NE of Payson	7,500′	trout
Woods Canyon Lake	34 miles NE of Payson	7,500′	rainbow trout

EASTERN ARIZONA

Name of Lake	Location	Elevation	Kinds of Fish
Becker Lake	2 miles W of Springerville	7,000′	rainbows (limited*)

Limited in the number of fish that you can catch, and size.

EASTERN ARIZONA (Continued)

Name of Lake	Location	Elevation	Kinds of Fish
Big Lake	25 miles SE of McNary (some unpaved road)	9,400′	trout
Crescent Lake	23 miles SE of McNary (some unpaved road)	9,000′	trout
Luna Lake	3 miles S of Alpine	7,900′	trout
Lyman Lake	11 miles S of St. Johns	5,900′	bass, channel catfish, northern pike, some trout, walleye
Rainbow Lake	½ mile W of Lakeville	6,800′	bass, bluegill, channel catfish, trout, walleye
Show Low Lake	4 miles S of Show Low, off Highway 260	6,500′	bass, bullheads, channel catfish, trout, walleye
White Mountain Lake	10 miles N of Show Low	5,700′	bass, bluegill, channel catfish, rainbow trout

SOUTHERN ARIZONA

Name of Lake	Location	Elevation	Kinds of Fish
Arivaca Lake	64 miles S of Tucson	3,750′	bass, bluegill, redear
Parker Canyon Lake	32 miles SE of Sonoita	5,200′	bass, bluegill, channel catfish, trout

SOUTHERN ARIZONA (Continued)

Name of Lake	Location	Elevation	Kinds of Fish
Patagonia Lake	16 miles NE of Nogales, AZ, Highway 82 (some unpaved road)	——	——
Pena Blanca Lake	17 miles NW of Nogales, AZ	4,000′	bass, bluegill, channel catfish, crappie, rainbow trout (in season)
Roper Lake	4 miles S of Safford	3,000′	bass, bluegill, channel catfish

WESTERN ARIZONA

Name of Lake	Location	Elevation	Kinds of Fish
Alamo Lake	38 miles N of Wenden	1,100′	bass, bluegill, catfish
Lake Havasu	Lake Havasu City	450′	bass, bluegill, channel catfish crappie
Imperial Reservoir	20 miles N of Yuma	200′	bass, bluegill, catfish, crappie
Martinez Lake	35 miles N of Yuma	200′	bass, bluegill, channel catfish, crappie
Lake Mead	77 miles NW of Kingman	1,130′	bass, channel catfish, bluegill, crappie, trout
Lake Mohave	——	650′	bass, bluegill, crappie, trout
Painted Rock Lake	34 miles NW of Gila Bend	735′	bass, bluegill, carp, catfish, goldfish, green sunfish

WATERCRAFT & BOAT ENGINE RESTRICTIONS

Power boats on the following Arizona waters are restricted to the use of a single electric motor only:

Arivaca Lake
Bear Canyon Lake
Becker Lake
Black Canyon Lake
Bunch Reservoir
Cluff Ponds
Coconino Reservoir
Concho Lake
Dogtown Reservoir
Granite Basin Lake
J.D. Lake
Knoll Lake
Lee Valley Lake
Lynx Lake
Nelson Reservoir
Pena Blanca Lake
Riggs Flat Lake
River Reservoir

CHAPTER 10

PARKS IN ARIZONA

Arizona can be justifiably proud of its State Park System. Most have ample facilities. The State Parks prove that Arizona is much more that just desert for many of the parks are located in National Forests amid huge acres of verdant land. For simplification purposes, we have divided the state into areas.

MID-CENTRAL REGION

Dead Horse Ranch

In beautiful Verde Valley, near Camp Verde, this State Park is only 320 acres. However, it has campsites with hook-ups, showers, picnicking and fishing.

Fort Verde State Historical Park

This famous spot in history is open all year and is located near the above Dead Horse Ranch. In the 1870's it was a staging area for the Federal cavalry during the famous Indian Campaigns. The park has a museum and a picnic area.

Lost Dutchman

Not far from Apache Junction, the park has only 300 acres (small when compared to others listed in this chapter). It has picnic tables, rest rooms and a primitive camping area.

McFarland State Historic Park

This State Park mainly consists of the adobe structure which was, in fact, the first Pinal County courthouse. The Museum, open all year, depicts Arizona history and law. The closest city is Florence.

EAST CENTRAL ARIZONA

Lyman Lake State Park

This State Park is located near the headwaters of the Little Colorado River. On the map, it is north of Springerville and south of St. Johns. Again, it is small by Arizona standards — only 160 acres. However, one can enjoy boating, swimming, water skiing and all-year fishing. The campgrounds have hook-ups, showers, ramadas and a store that sells fishing supplies and food.

WEST CENTRAL ARIZONA

Alamo Lake

Thirty-eight miles from Welden (north) off US 60. You have to drive over a blacktop road part of the way. The Army Corp of Engineers built this 500-acre recreational lake, which has picnicing, water sports, hiking trails, fishing and hunting in specific areas. It also has primitive campsites, some hook-up sites and a boat launch ramp.

Buckskin Mountain

Eleven miles north of Parker on Arizona 95. The State Park juts out into the Colorado River. It is a favorite of water sport enthusiasts. Facilities include a beach, swimming, boat launch ramp, picnicing and restrooms with showers.

Lake Havasu

In Lake Havasu City, with 45 miles of shore line. Visitors can enjoy resort style facilities or rough it at a lakeside camp. Mostly famous for water-oriented facilities. The region is divided as follows:

Pittsburg Point: Just west of Lake Havasu City across from world famous London Bridge. Here you can enjoy golf, tennis and trailer parks, motels, campgrounds and boating facilities.

Windsor Beach: North of famed London Bridge; it offers a good beach, swimming, picnic areas and a boat launching ramp.

Cattail Cove: Fifteen miles south of Lake Havasu City and one mile west off Arizona 95. It has campsites with hook-ups, showers, picnic areas and boating facilities. However, you must come in by boat to take advantage of the campsite facilities.

SOUTHWESTERN ARIZONA

Yuma Territorial Prison

Yuma. Although closed in 1876 after only 33 years of operation, it was one of the best known prisons in the West. There are great glimpses of what convict life was a century ago. See the Chapter on Arts and Craft Museums.

Painted Rock State Historical Park

Accessible only from I-8, some 15 miles west of Gila Bend, then about 12 miles north on Painted Rock Road. Father Kino, pioneers, immigrants and stage coach riders all once traversed here. There is a primitive campsite, but no toilet facilities.

For information on the following County Parks in the region, contact Yuma County Chamber of Commerce, 200 West First Street, Yuma, Arizona 85364: Adair Park, Butterfield Park, Friendship Park and Gadsden Park.

SOUTHEASTERN ARIZONA

Picacho Peak

This historic site, scene of the only Civil War skirmish fought on Arizona soil, is about an hour drive from Tucson (north toward Phoenix on I-10). There is both primitive and RV camping here, nature walks and hiking trails. One such hiking trail leads to the summit — 1,500′ above the desert floor.

Roper Lake

South of Safford. You can sit by the water's edge, picnic or swim in the 30-acre lake. The boating here is restricted to oars or electric motors.

Patagonia Lake

In Patagonia, south of Tucson. Many fisherman talk about this State Park because the coves swarm with panfish, and catfish flourish in the main body of the lake. There is a large picnic area here; a marina, swimming beach, launch ramp and dock. You can rent boats and canoes.

PHOENIX AREA PARKS

The Phoenix parks system is divided into 5 districts. The following is a list of the main administrative office and the five district offices. Call for a current calendar of park events, and locations nearest you.

Phoenix Department of Parks & Recreations
Administrative Office
125 E. Washington Avenue
Phoenix, AZ 85004
262-6861

Northwest District Office
Dept. of Parks & Recreation
3901 W. Glendale
262-7675

Northeast District Office
Dept. of Parks & Recreation
334 E. Caron
Phoenix, AZ
262-6696

Eastern District Office
Dept. of Parks & Recreation
1430 S. 26th Street
Phoenix, AZ
262-7714

Southern District Office
Dept. of Parks & Recreation
227 E. Cody Drive
Phoenix, AZ
262-6486

Western District Office
Dept. of Parks & Recreation
2700 N. 15th Avenue
Phoenix, AZ 262-4539

There are six large "desert-mountain" parks in or adjoining Phoenix and Scottsdale which are ideal for hiking, mountain-climbing and picnicking. Taking the largest one first, they are:

South Mountain Park: Covering 14,817 acres of desert and mountain, with 10 miles of paved roads and 40 miles of horse trails, this is the largest municipal park in the world. Facilities include many picnic ramadas, cement dance pavilions, play areas, restrooms and look-out points from which you have a superb view of the Valley of the Sun.

There is an entrance fee of 25¢ per car, and the park is open from 8 a.m. to midnight daily. To reach, drive south on Central Avenue. Famous as a "Lover's Lane."

Papago Park: Situated in between Phoenix and Scottsdale (6000 East Van Buren), Papago Park has something for almost everybody; riding stables, a golf course, hiking trails, lighted picnic areas, barbecue grills, play areas, an indoor smallbore firing range, and a marvelous view of Phoenix lights at night. Size: 889 acres.

Squaw Peak Park: Just a mile off Glendale Avenue/Lincoln Drive (turn north at the 2300 east block in the center of the Indian Wells residential area) Squaw Peak Park has 546 acres, most of which are made up of deep ravines and a series of ridges and peaks overlooking Phoenix and Paradise Valley.

There are fireplaces, picnic ramadas, water, restroom facilities, horse-hitch racks and several miles of hiking, climbing and riding trails — all of them providing excellent views of the surrounding Valleys.

North Mountain Park: Smallest of the six parks (275 acres) this attractive northside recreational area overlooks central Phoenix, and has the usual picnic facilities and climbing trails, plus a playground for children. To reach go north on 7th Street on through Sunnyslope, to just beyond Mountain View Road. The park is on the west side as 7th Street climbs up the mountain pass toward Moon Valley.

Thunderbird Park: In the Hedgepeth Hills 10 miles north of Glendale (which adjoins Phoenix on the west) on 59th Avenue, the Thunderbird Park has water, restrooms, dance pavilions, picnic ramadas and fireplaces for barbecuing. The area totals 1,000 acres.

Estrella Mountain Park: Located on Bullard Road off Highway 80 near Goodyear, the Estrella Park includes picnic areas, playgrounds, ramadas, fireplaces, nature trails and an 18-hole golf course with clubhouse. The park is 1,825 acres big.

Individual ramadas and picnic tables can be reserved at no cost for group picnics and parties at the four closest desert parks. For reservations at North Mountain, Squaw Peak and South Mountain Parks, call 276-2221.

RED MOUNTAIN RECREATION PARK

Maintained by the Salt River Indian tribe, it is located just above Granite Reef Dam along the banks of the Verde. To reach, drive east on McDowell Road or Shea Blvd. to Bee Line Highway, and turn left. Proceed on until you reach turn-off signs as you approach the river, and go left or right, along the banks of the Verde.

There are picnic tables and some grills, and swimming "holes" every few hundred feet. The Verde can get quite low during mid-summer. If you want more water, continue on right for about a mile from the main highway to where the Verde and the larger Salt River join. There is a fee of $1 per car, collected at a roadside stand after your turn off the main highway.

CHAPTER 11

ROCKHOUNDING

Arizona is one of the most mineralized areas on the surface of the planet, and is thus a "rockhounder's" paradise. Rockhounding is in fact often listed as *the* leading recreational activity in the state.

Many of Arizona's "Rockhounds" meet at Round-Ups and Shows all across the state. There one can meet not only those who collect rocks and minerals, but many who polish their beautiful agates, jaspers and the like.

We have listed at the end of this chapter many of Arizona's Rockhound Clubs (Earth Science Clubs). Changes do occur, however, so it would be wise to write to the people who provided us with this list. For a current update: Curator, Arizona Mineral Museum, State Fairgrounds, 19th Avenue & McDowell, Phoenix, Az 85007.

HOW ROCKS ARE RECOGNIZED & CLASSIFIED

By dcfinition, rocks are usually composed of two or more minerals. The proportions of the different minerals making up the rock may vary — even the combination of minerals may change within rocks of the same name. Therefore, rocks are classified by method of formation. The three classifications of rocks are igneous, sedimentary and metamorphic.

Igneous rocks are formed by the cooling of a one-time molten mass. They contain no fossils.

Sedimentary rocks are made up of fragments from other rocks, formed of layers of gravel, sand or clay. Two famous examples of this kind of rock are shale and limestone.

Metamorphic rocks are those that have been changed or altered from the form in which they were orginally laid down. In general these rocks show bands of light and dark minerals.

MAP & LEGEND

See the Map below to check out which counties in Arizona have which minerals. Each number corresponds to a county.

Counties on Map (by number)

1. Mohave
2. Coconino
3. Navajo
4. Apache
5. Gila
6. Yavapai
7. Yuma
8. Maricopa
9. Pinal
10. Graham
11. Greenlee
12. Cochise
13. Pima
14. Santa Cruz

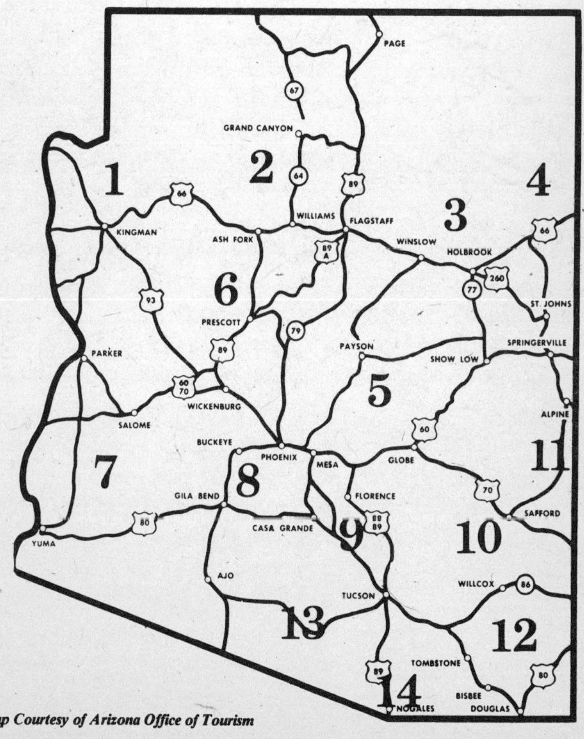

Map Courtesy of Arizona Office of Tourism

NAME OF MINERAL	COUNTIES WHERE FOUND (See map for number)
Actinolite	1, 6, 7, 9, 10, 11, 12, 13, 14
Agate	1 through 13
Amethyst	1, 5, 8, 14
Amphibole	5, 6, 7, 9, 11, 12, 13
Analcime	6
Apache Tears	1, 6, 8, 9
Arag onite	7, 12, 13
Asbestos (chrysotile)	5, 9 11, 12
Azurite	5, 6, 7, 8, 9, 11, 12, 13
Barite	1, 5, 6, 7, 8, 9, 10, 12, 13
Beryl	1, 6, 7, 8, 13
Biotite (Mica)	Widespread through state, no specific county
Bornite	1, 2, 5, 6, 7, 8, 9, 12, 13
Calcite	1, 5, 6, 9, 12, 14
Carnotite	3, 4, 5, 6
Chalcanthite	1, 5, 6, 8, 9, 11, 12, 13
Chalcedony	Found in every county
Chalcocite	1, 5, 6, 7, 8, 9, 10, 11, 12, 13, 14
Chalcopyrite	1, 3, 5, 6, 7, 8, 9, 10, 11, 12, 13, 14
Chrysolla	1, 5, 6, 7, 8, 9, 11
Cinnabar	1, 5, 6, 7, 8, 9, 13
Copper	1, 5, 6, 9, 11, 12, 13
Cuprite	1, 5, 6, 7, 8, 9, 11, 12, 13, 14
Dioptase	5, 6, 9, 11
Dolomite	2, 6, 7, 11, 12, 13
Epidote	1, 5, 6, 7, 8, 10, 11, 12, 13, 14
Feldspar	1, 5, 6, 7, 8, 9, 13
Fluorite	1, 5, 6, 7, 8, 10, 11
Galena	1, 5, 6, 7, 8, 9, 10, 12, 13, 14
Garnet	1, 2, 4, 5, 6, 7, 8, 10
Goethite	1, 5, 6, 7, 8, 9, 10, 12, 13, 14
Gold	1, 5, 6, 7, 8, 9, 10 11, 12, 13, 14
Gypsum	1, 3, 6, 7, 8, 9, 11, 13

Hematite	1, 2, 5, 6, 7, 8, 9, 12
Jasper	1, 3, 4, 5, 6, 7, 8 9, 10, 11, 13, 14
Kyantie	7, 8
Magnetitie	1, 2, 5, 6, 7, 8, 11, 13, 14
Marble	5, 7, 8, 11, 12
Muscovite (Mica)	6, 7
Olivine	4, 5
Onyx (Mexican)	1, 2, 5, 6, 7, 8, 14
Opal	1, 5, 6, 7, 8, 12
Peridot	4, 5
Petrified Wood	1, 2, 3, 4, 5, 7, 9, 12
Pyrite	1, 5, 6, , 8, 9, 11, 12, 13, 14
Pyrolusite	1, 6, 7, 8, 11, 12, 14
Pyroxene	3, 5, 7, 9, 12, 13
Quartz	1, 5, 6, 7, 9, 10, 12, 13, 14
Rose Quartz	1, 8
Scheelite	1, 6, 7, 8, 9, 10, 12, 13, 14
Serpentine	2, 5, 9, 11, 12
Siderite	1, 5, 6, 7, 11, 12, 13
Silver	1, 5, 6, 8, 9, 10, 12, 14
Sphalerite	1, 5, 6, 9, 10, 11, 12, 13, 14
Tourmaline	1, 2, 6, 7, 8, 9, 13, 14
Tremolite	6, 7, 8, 10, 12, 14
Turquoise	1, 5, 8, 9, 12, 13, 14
Uraninite	2, 3, 4, 5, 6
Vanadinite	1, 5, 6, 7, 8, 9, 12, 13
Willemite	5, 9, 11, 12, 13
Wulfenite	1, 5, 7, 8, 9, 10, 12, 13, 14

ROCKHOUND CLUBS (EARTH SCIENCE CLUBS)

The following list of Earth Science Clubs has been divided into geographic area. See the reference at the beginning of the chapter for up-to-date information on these Clubs. (We have listed only those Clubs open to new membership.)

Phoenix Metropolitan Area

Glen Rockers
6817 W. San Miguel
Glendale, AZ 85303

Maricopa Lapidary Society
P.O. Box 1225
Phoenix, AZ 85252

Mineralogical Society of Arizona
P.O. Box 902
Phoenix, AZ

Roadrunners
P.O. Box 163
Mesa, AZ 85204

Stoneagers
Mineral Building
State Fairgrounds
Phoenix, AZ 85007

Y.M.C.A. Rockhound Club
350 North First Avenue
Phoenix, AZ 85003

Other Cities (listed by alphabetical order)

Apache Junction Rock & Gem Club, Inc.
Apache Junction, AZ 85220

Bisbee Mineral Club
Box 284
Bisbee, AZ 85603

Flagstaff Gem & Mineral Society
P.O. Box 1261
Flagstaff, AZ 86002

Gila County Gem & Mineral Society
413 Live Oak
Miami, AZ 85539

Gila Valley Gem & Mineral Society
Safford, AZ 85546

Lake Havasu Gem & Mineral Society
P.O. Box 990
Lake Havasu City, AZ 86003

Mohave County Gemstoners
P.O. Box 281
Kingman, AZ 86401

Mingus Gem & Mineral Society
P.O. Box 1040
Cottonwood, AZ 86326

Mohave Rancho Rock Club
P.O. Box 294
Dolan Springs, AZ 86441

Oak Creek Gem & Mineral Society
P.O. Box 505
Sedona, AZ 86336

Quartzsite Roadrunner Gem & Mineral Club
P.O. Box 338
Quartzsite, AZ 85346

Scottsdale Gem & Mineral Society
Scottsdale, AZ 85251

Silvery Colorado River Rock Club
P.O. Box 2648
Riviera, AZ 86442

Sunsites Gem & Mineral Club
P.O.Box 87
Pearce, AZ 85625

Tucson Gem & Mineral Society, Inc.
P.O. Box 42543
Tucson, AZ 85713

White Mountain Gem & Mineral Club
Show Low, AZ 85929

Wickenburg Gem & Mineral Society
P.O. Box 1614
Wickenburg, AZ 85358

Yavapai Rockhound Club
Singletree & Lariat Lane
Camp Wood Route
Prescott, AZ 86307

CHAPTER 12

SIGHTSEEING AT CLASSIC HOTELS

Arizona has some of the finest classic resorts and hotels in the country. Even if you cannot afford to stay at such places, they are worth a visit to stroll around the grounds and to see the interior settings.

Bisbee: Copper Queen Hotel

Bisbee, only 94 miles southeast of Tucson, has been called Queen of the Copper Mine Camp. It has retained its flavor of Western frontier and mining town. In fact, history walks beside you in this mile high city. In 1877, rowdy, brawling miners came to mine the rich copper lode. This heritage molded the character of Bisbee in yesteryear and it still exists today.

The famous *Copper Queen Hotel* was built in 1902 by the Copper Queen Mining Company, and combines grandeur, charm and comfort. Its guests over the years have included such luminaries as Teddy Roosevelt and "Black Jack" Pershing who pursued Pancho Villa, the Mexican revolutionary in a futile chase. Later Pershing commanded all the U.S. forces in World War I.

In those early days, the saloon at the Copper Queen was a meeting place for officials and politicos. Arizona was still a decade away from statehood.

The Copper Queen is still undergoing a program to restore it to its original grandeur. As of this writing, it has 42 refurbished rooms and two attractive lobbies. A visit to the Copper Queen Saloon in the hotel is a trip back in time to nostalgic days.

The Bucky O'Neil dining room, named after one of Teddy

Roosevelt's first Rough Riders, accommodates 50 persons.

The outside decor of the hotel is the essence of simplicity. The hotel also boasts a sidewalk cafe, a heated swimming pool and the only four-story elevator in Bisbee.

Douglas: The Gadsen Hotel

Douglas, some 122 miles to the southeast of Tucson, also was noted for its lawless days. The present site of Douglas was a popular meeting ground for cowboys who worked cattle in the area in the 1880's and 1890's. But the town was most famous for copper mining.

The Gadsen Hotel was built in 1907 when people like Wyatt Earp and Pancho Villa were still slinging guns and making headlines. The hotel was named for James Gadsen, the U.S. minister to Mexico in 1854 who negotiated the deal that gave the U.S. a huge slice of Mexican territory.

So much of history was made at the Gadsen Hotel that it was declared a National Historic Site in 1976. This is a fitting tribute to this stately five story, 160 room structure.

The hotel is unique. The spacious main lobby is elegantly set with a solid white Italian marble staircase and four soaring marble columns. Each of the columns is decorated in 14 karat gold leaf. In 1929 when a fire gutted the hotel's original wooden frame, each column was appraised at $20,000.

To add brightness and color, two authentic Tiffany vaulted skylights run the length of the lobby. A beautiful stained glass mural extends some 42 feet across one wall of the large mezzanine. It all blends together in such a way to make even a Hollywood set designer green with envy.

Before leaving the hotel, look at the El Conquistador Dining Room with its Spanish-style decor and Old World elegance. There is a series of colorful murals hanging from the walls, their origins unknown, adding to the mystique of the hotel. Address is 1046 G Avenue.

Grand Canyon National Park: El Tovar

This majestic 100-room hotel was opened in January 1905 to accommodate travelers from the Santa Fe railroad. Built of native boulders and Oregon pine, the hotel was named in honor of the Spanish explorer Pedro de Tovar who led the first expedition to Hopi Indian country in 1540.

El Tovar was designed to blend in with the Grand Canyon environment, and a visit here proves that this goal was certainly attained. Nothing was spared to make the El Tovar one of the great hotels of its era. The building was completely equipped with electric lights powered by its own steam generator. Fresh water was brought in on railroad tank cars from Del Rio, 120 miles away. They even grew fresh vegetables and fresh fruits in their own greenhouse in those early days.

Most of the original wood is still visible and makes up the exterior, the flooring and walls. The architect had the outside logs and wooden shingles stained, so even today, El Tovar maintains its wonderfully rustic look. The floors creaked when this great hotel opened and they still do today.

Walk down the narrow halls. Visit the Rendezvous Room with its bulky rafters, and the warm, atmospheric Dining Room with its huge fireplace.

The Fred Harvey Company has run the hotel since it opened. In 1905 a suite was only $8.00 a day; today it costs nearly $100!

Phoenix: The Arizona Biltmore

In 1981 the *Arizona Biltmore* won the prestigious Mobil 5-Star award for the 22nd consecutive year. No other hotel or resort in the entire country can make that claim.

Arizona Biltmore is set in the foothills of Squaw Peak. It is surrounded by lush landscaping, including gorgeous flower gardens, palm trees and cactus.

The architect and builder was Albert Chase McArthur who once worked for Frank Lloyd Wright. The Wright influence is seen almost everywhere. The lobby itself has been called a "mini-oasis," a freestanding cluster of columns, plants and charming waterfall.

Completed in 1929, the Biltmore was sold to William Wrigley, the chewing gum millionaire. It changed hands again in 1973 when Talley Industries purchased it. Today it is owned by a Canadian investment group.

Other highlights of the hotel include:

The Gold Room: Old World charm at its best. The gold leaf ceiling is from the original 1929 design. The murals inside the

room are striking; while the decor is elegant.
The Aztec Lounge: Adjacent to the foyer, shows the strong influence of Frank Lloyd Wright. Light filters through the skylight ceiling and makes the room glow.
The Orangerie: A restaurant with stalacite chandeliers built in 1973. There are also magnificent ballrooms and conference facilities. Address: 24th Street and Missouri Avenue.

Tucson: Arizona Inn

The *Arizona Inn* in present-day Tucson was the dream of Isabella Greenway, a wealthy socialite. She created this spacious classic country resort to have a place for the unusual furniture she had manufactured but had trouble marketing. In addition to her new furniture, she used her own family heirlooms to decorate the place, including antiques and Mexican-American works of art.

The Arizona Inn opened in 1930 and bears no resemblance to some of the austere, high-rise structures of the period. The overall feeling about the Inn is one of warmth. The units are made of soft coral highlighted by shutters with a Williamsburg blue trim. The rooms are all intimate, with Western style touches.

The library is really a decorator's dream. It is huge with high ceilings, a Moroccan rug, a fireplace and several long white couches.

There are 86 rooms in this cottage style resort, not big by today's standards. However, the Arizona Inn has attracted some of the world's most famous people. Guests have included Sir Winston Churchill, Salvadore Dali, the Duke and Duchess of Windsor and Cary Grant, the movie actor.

When the Arizona Inn opened in 1930 it was a desert resort, but Tucson has grown so fast, it is now part of the city. The Arizona Inn, all 14 acres, defies the thrust of modern day bigness and time.

CHAPTER 13

SPORTS ACTIVITIES

With its virtually year-around dry, sunny climate, Arizona is a sportsman's paradise. The bright sunshine that is typical of both summer and winter beckons all ages outside to join in on the fun and games — which range from flying kites and frisbees to softball, baseball, tennis, bicycling and hiking to square dancing.

When planning to utilize school grounds or school gyms check to see if the schools are in session.

Mesa

Baseball - Softball
Lighted Fields - Softball

Name of Field	Location	# of Fields	Rest rooms
Eisenhower	300 E. 8th Street	1	No
Elsworth Park	850 E. 2nd Avenue	2	Yes
Evergreen Park	328 W. 2nd Avenue	2	Yes
Escobedo	514 N. Hibbert	1	No
Jefferson School	308 S. Jefferson	1	No
Kleinman Park	850 W. 8th Avenue	1	No
Lincoln	50 E. 10th Street	1	No
Mesa Central High School	361 S. Center	2	Yes

Name of Field	Location	# of Fields	Rest rooms
Powell Jr. High School	924 S. Extension	1	No
Riverview	2700 W. 8th Street	4	Yes
Westwood High School	650 N Extension	2	Yes

Lighted Fields - Baseball

Carson Jr. High School	655 N. Extension	1	Yes
Fitch Park	650 N. Center	3	Yes
HoHokam Park	1250 N Center	1	Yes
Jefferson	306 S. Jefferson	1	Yes
Mesa Jr. High School	850 E. 2nd Avenue	1	Yes
Westwood High School	650 N. Extension	1	Yes

Basketball - Open Gyms

Generally, the availability period is from early June until the end of July.
The following schools participate:
Mesa High School; Mountainview; Rhodes; Westwood.

Outdoor Basketball at Parks

Name of Park	Address
Chapparal	1645 N. Gilbert
Country Side	1120 S. 32nd Street
Dobson ranch	2363 S. Dobson
Fitch Park	850 N Central
Pioneer	326 E. Main

Racquetball

Several courts at Fitch Park, 650 N. Center, but on a reservation basis **only.** Also, all the outdoor courts at high schools in Mesa can be used for Racquetball. Mesa Community College also has facilities. Take the Superstition Freeway, Route 360, toward Mesa and exit at Dobson. You will see signs to the college.

Tennis Courts	Lighted	Unlighted	Total
Carson Jr. High - 525 N. Westwood		2	2
Dobson Ranch - 2155 S. Dobson Road	3		3
Fremont Jr. High - 1001 N. Bush Highway	2	2	4
HoHokam - 1235 N. Center	17 (1 practice)		17
Kino Jr. High - 848 N. Horne	4		4
Kleinman Park - 710 S. Extension Road	8		8
Mesa Central High School - 15 W. 2nd Ave.	3	3	6
Mesa Cmnty College - 1833 W. Southern	6	2	8
Mesa Jr. High School - 828 E. Broadway	4		4

	Lighted	Unlighted	Total
Mesa High School - 1630 E. Southern	6		6
Mountain View H.S. - 2700 E. Brown	6		6
Poston Jr. High School - 2433 E. Adobe		4	4
Powell Jr. High School - 855 W. 8th Ave.	4		4
Rhodes Jr. H.S. - 1860 S. Longmore		6	6
Westwood High School - 945 W. 8th Street	4	4	8

Phoenix

Phoenix is justly proud of its District Park System, consisting of EAST DISTRICT (administrative offices at 1430 S. 26th St); NORTHEAST DISTRICT (office at 334 E. Caron); NORTHWEST DISTRICT (3901 W. Glendale); and WEST DISTRICT (2700 N. 15th Avenue). Each District serves from 100,000 to 200,000 people. The crowded urban environment is thus broken by large recreational areas covering several hundred acres.

Bicycle Paths

Phoenix offers bicycle enthusiasts many miles of bike trails. Most of these bike paths wind through parks and picnic areas; skirt desert scenes and follow picturesque tree-lined canal banks. Phoenix has developed three paths: the 11.3 mile *Highline,* the 22.6 mile *Arizona Loop* and the 13.6 mile *Papago Loop.* Together, they comprise 47 miles of smooth, uninterrupted routes.

For more information about these bike paths and their exact locations, contact: City of Phoenix, Parks, Recreation & Library Division, 125 E. Washington St., Phoenix, AZ 85004. Telephone: 262-6861.

Recommended reading: *Bicyclists Guide to Arizona,* (Phoenix Books/Publishers, P.O. Box 32008, Phoenix, AZ 85064. $4.95.) A fine book about bicycling in Arizona. For those who enjoy short rides, medium rides, or long rides. In author, Peter L. Bower's own words: "Places like Clint's Wells, Nowhere, Sunflower and Skull Valley are only dots on the map to those in a hurry to reach a destination. But on a bicycle a destination is only an excuse to experience the effort and thrill of the journey."

Department of Parks and Recreation

Main Administration Office: 125 E. Washington St.
Phoenix, AZ 85001
Tel: 262-6861

Eastern District Office:	1430 S. 26th St. Phoenix, AZ 85034 Tel: 262-7714
Northeast District Office:	334 E. Caron Phoenix, AZ 85020 Tel: 262-6696
Northwest District Office:	3901 W. Glendale Ave. Phoenix, AZ 85019 Tel: 262-6575
Southern District Office:	227 E. Cody Drive Phoenix, AZ 85040 Tel: 262-6486
Western District Office:	2700 N. 15th Ave. Phoenix, AZ 85007 Tel: 262-4548

Parks

Please note that while daytime use of ball fields in the Phoenix park system is free, the city is now charging a fee for nighttime use when lights are required. Call the district office of the park you want to use for the latest information.

Acoma - 39th Avenue and Acoma Road
- Area lighting
- Football field
- Parking lot

Alicia - 2021 W. Alicia Avenue
- 2 basketball courts
- 2 football/soccer fields

Cactus - 3801 W. Cactus
- Area lighting
- 1 softball/baseball field
- 1 exercise trail
- 3 football/soccer fields
- Parking lot
- Playground apparatus
- Recreation building
- Restrooms

Conocido - 31st Avenue & Paradise Lane
- Exercise trail

Cortez - 35th Avenue & Dunlap Avenue
- Area lighting
- 2 ball fields
- 1 basketball court
- Bleachers
- Parking lot
- Restrooms

Country Gables - 32nd Drive and Banff Lane
- Area lighting
- 1 basketball court
- Playground apparatus

La Pradera - 39th Avenue and Glendale Avenue
- Area lighting
- Exercise trail
- 2 football/soccer fields
- Parking lot

Mariposa - 3202 W. Morton Avenue
- 1 softball/baseball field
- 1 basketball court
- 1 football/soccer field
- Restrooms

Mountain View - 7th Avenue & Peoria Avenue
- Area lighting
- 1 football field
- Parking lot
- Drinking fountain

Royal Palm - 15th Avenue & Butler Drive
- Exercise trail
- Drinking fountain
- Parking lot

Solano - 5625 N. 17th Avenue
- Area lighting
- 1 softball/baseball field
- 1 basketball court
- 1 football/soccer field
- Restrooms

Washington - 23rd Avenue & Maryland Avenue
- Area lighting
- 2 softball/baseball fields
- 1 basketball court
- Bleachers
- Exercise trail
- Restrooms

Westown - 33rd Avenue & Corrine Drive
1 softball/baseball field
1 football/soccer field
Bleachers
Restrooms
Drinking fountain

West Plaza - 43rd Avenue & Maryland Avenue
Area lighting
Drinking fountain

Northeast District

(We have not mentioned some parks in this district because they lack sports facilities)

Palma - 12th Street & Dunlap Avenue
Area lighting
3 softball/baseball fields
1 basketball court
Bleachers
1 football/soccer field
Parking lot
Restrooms

Sereno - 56th Street & Sweetwater
Area lighting
2 softball/baseball fields
2 basketball courts
Parking lot

Sunnyslope Community Center Park - 802 E. Vogel Avenue
Area lighting
1 basketball court
Horseshoe court
Parking lot
Restrooms
Drinking fountain

Western District

Alkire - 17th Avenue & Papago
Area lighting
1 softball/baseball field
Bleachers
Restrooms

Cielito - 3402 W. Campbell
Area lighting
2 softball/baseball fields
1 football/soccer field
Parking lot

Coffelt - 1510 S. 10th Drive
- Area lighting
- 1 softball/baseball field
- 1 basketball court
- Bleachers
- Restrooms

El Oso - 75th Avenue & Osborn Road
- Area lighting
- 3 softball/baseball fields
- Bleachers
- 2 football/soccer fields
- Parking lot
- Drinking fountain

Encanto - 15th Avenue & Encanto Blvd.
- Archery range
- Area lighting
- 2 softball/baseball fields
- 1 basketball court
- Bleachers
- 2 football/soccer fields
- Horseshoe courts
- Parking lot
- Restrooms
- Drinking fountain

Falcon - 35th Avenue & Roosevelt Street
- Area lighting
- 3 softball/baseball fields
- 1 basketball court
- Bleachers
- Parking lot
- Drinking fountain

Holiday - 67th Avenue & Minnezona Avenue
- Area lighting
- 1 softball/baseball field
- 1 basketball court
- 1 football/soccer field
- Parking lot
- Restrooms
- Drinking fountain

Marivue - 55 Avenue & Osborn Road
- Area lighting
- 2 softball/baseball fields
- 1 basketball court
- Bleachers
- 1 football/soccer field
- Parking lot
- Restrooms
- Drinking fountain

Maryvale - 51st Avenue & Campbell
- 1 softball/baseball field
- 1 football/soccer field
- Parking lot
- Restrooms

Orme - 47th Avenue & Osborn
- 1 basketball court
- 2 football/soccer fields

Smith - 41st Avenue & Grant
- 1 softball/baseball field
- 1 basketball court
- Bleachers
- 1 football/soccer field
- 1 volleyball court
- Restrooms
- Drinking fountain

Starlight - 7810 W. Osborn
- Area lighting
- 1 softball/baseball field
- 1 basketball court
- Bleachers
- Shuffleboard court
- Parking lot
- Restrooms
- Drinking fountain

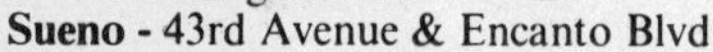

Sueno - 43rd Avenue & Encanto Blvd.
- Area lighting
- 1 football/soccer field
- Parking lot

University - 10th Avenue & Van Buren Street
- 2 softball/baseball fields
- 1 basketball court
- 1 football/ soccer field
- Parking lot
- Drinking fountain

Willow - 28th Avenue & Polk Street
1 softball/baseball field
Bleachers
1 football/soccer field

Eastern District

Berney - 20th Street & Lincoln
Area lighting
1 softball/baseball field
Bleachers
1 football/soccer field
Parking lot
Restrooms
Drinking fountain

Central - First Street & Tonto Street
Area lighting
1 softball/baseball field
1 basketball court
Bleachers
Restrooms
Drinking fountain

Coronado - 12th Street & Coronado Road
Area lighting
2 softball/baseball fields
1 basketball court
Bleachers
2 football/soccer fields
Parking lot
Restrooms
Drinking fountain

Eastlake - 16th Street & Jefferson
Area lighting
1 softball/baseball field
2 basketball courts
Bleachers
1 football/soccer field
2 shuffleboard courts
Parking lot
Restrooms
Drinking fountain

Edison - 19th Street & Roosevelt Street
Area lighting
1 softball/baseball field
1 basketball court
Restrooms
Drinking fountain

Grant - 701 S. Third Avenue
- Area lighting
- 1 softball/baseball field
- 1 basketball court
- Bleachers
- 1 football/soccer field
- Restrooms

Green Valley Park - 14th Street & Watkins Road
- Area lighting
- 1 softball/baseball field
- 1 basketball court
- 1 football/soccer field
- Parking lot
- Restrooms

Harmon Park - 5th Avenue & Yavapai Street
- Area lighting
- 3 softball/baseball fields
- 2 basketball courts
- Bleachers
- 1 football/soccer field
- 1 horseshoe court
- Parking lot
- Restrooms
- Drinking fountain

Madison - 16th Street & Glenrosa
- 4 softball/baseball fields
- 1 basketball court
- Bleachers
- 2 football/soccer fields
- 4 shuffleboard courts
- Parking lot
- Restrooms
- Drinking fountain

Monterey - 350 E. Oak Street
- 2 softball/baseball fields
- 1 basketball court
- 1 football/soccer field
- Restrooms
- Drinking fountain

Nuestro - 9th Street & Pima Street
- Area lighting
- 1 softball/baseball field
- 1 basketball court
- Bleachers
- Restrooms
- Drinking fountain

Papago - Van Buren Street & Galvin Parkway
4 basketball courts
Bleachers
Restrooms
Drinking fountain

Perry - 2700 N. 32nd Street
Area lighting
1 softball/baseball field
1 basketball court
Bleachers
2 football/soccer fields
Parking lot
Restrooms
Drinking fountain

Pierce - 2150 N. 46th Street
Area lighting
2 softball/baseball fields
1 basketball court
Bleachers
2 football/soccer fields
Parking lot
Restrooms
Drinking fountain

Southern District

El Prado - 6428 S. 19th Avenue
Area lighting
2 softball/baseball fields
1 basketball court
1 football/soccer field

El Reposo - 502 E. Alta Vista Road
Area lighting
1 softball/baseball field
1 basketball court
1 football/soccer field
1 volleyball court
Parking lot

Eteban - 32nd Street & Roeser Road
Area lighting
3 softball/baseball fields
1 basketball court
2 football/soccer fields
Parking lot
Restrooms
Drinking fountain

Hayden - 3rd Avenue & Tamarisk Street
Area lighting
2 softball/baseball fields
1 basketball court
Bleachers
1 football/soccer field
Parking lot
Restrooms
Drinking fountain

Lindo - 2200 W. Roeser Road
Area lighting
1 softball/baseball field
1 basketball court
1 football/soccer field
1 volleyball court
Parking lot
Restrooms
Drinking fountain

Nueve - 4418 S. 9th Street
Area lighting
1 softball/baseball field
1 basketball court
Bleachers
1 volleyball court
Parking lot
Restrooms
Drinking fountain

Okemah - 38th Street & Anne Street
Area lighting
1 softball/baseball field
1 basketball court
Bleachers
1 football/soccer field
1 volleyball court
Parking lot
Restrooms
Drinking fountain

Playa Marguarita - 36th Avenue & Roeser
Area lighting
1 softball/baseball field
1 basketball court
1 football/soccer field
Restrooms
Drinking fountain

Roesley - 15th Avenue & Romley Avenue
Area lighting
1 football/soccer field
South Mountain Park - 10919 S. Central Avenue
1 softball/baseball field
Parking lot
Restrooms
Drinking fountain

Lighted Tennis Facilities

East District

Coronado Park - 12th Street & Coronado. 2 courts.
Eastlake Park - 16th Street & Jefferson. 2 courts.
Granada Park - 20th Street & Maryland. 4 courts.
Harmon Park - 5th Avenue & Yavapai. 2 courts.
Herberger Park - 56th Street & Indian School Road. 4 courts.
Madison Park - 15th Street & Glenrosa. 2 courts.
Perry Park - 31st Street & E. Windsor. 2 courts.
Pierce Park - 2150 N. 46th Street. 4 courts.
Roadrunner Park - 35th Street & Cactus. 6 courts.
Verde Park - 9th Street & Polk. 2 courts.

South District

El Reposo Park - 5th Street & Alta Vista. 4 courts.
Esteban Park - 32nd Street & Roeser Road. 2 courts.
Nueve Park - 4418 S. 9th Street. 2 courts.

West District

Cielito Park - 35th Avenue & Campbell. 4 courts.
Encanto Park - 15th Avenue & Encanto Blvd. 8 courts.
Mariposa Park - 32nd Avenue & W. Morton. 4 courts.
Solano Park - 5625 N. 17th Avenue. 2 courts.
Starlight Park - 7810 W. Osborn Road. 2 courts.
Tennis Center - 6330 N. 21st Avenue. 22 courts.
University Park - 10th Avenue & Van Buren. 4 courts.

Scottsdale

Baseball/softball

Lighted fields
Eldorado Park - 2311 N Miller Road. 3 fields.
Vista Del Camino - 7700 E. Roosevelt. 1 field.

Basketball Courts

Outdoor and lighted

Paiute Park - 6535 E. Osborn. ½ court.
Pima Park - 8600 E. Thomas. 1 court.
Agualinda Park - Pima Road & McDonald Drive. 1 court.

Outdoor and unlit

Shoshone Park - 8300 Via Dorado. 1 court.
Comache Park - 7639 Via de los Ninos. 1 court.
Eldorado Park - 2311 N. Miller. 1 court.
Indian School Park - Indian School Rd. & Hayden Rd. 1 court.

Bikeway System

Scottsdale has one of the best planned bikeway systems in the Valley. A good map explains the entire route.

Contact:
City of Scottsdale
Public Information
3939 Civic Center Plaza
Scottsdale, AZ 85251
Telephone: 994-2436

Open Gyms

Chaparral High School - 6935 E. Gold Dust. June-July.
Coronado High School - 2501 N. 74th Street. June-August.
Saguaro High School - 6250 N. 82nd Street. June-August.
Scottsdale High School - 7410 E. Indian School Rd. June-July.
For the exact dates and hours available, call City of Scottsdale, Recreation Division. Telephone: 994-2436

Racquetball

You can only use the racquetball facilities when school is not in session.

Chaparral High School - 6935 E. Gold Dust
Coronado High School - 2501 N. 74th Street
Saguaro High School - 6250 N. 82nd Street
Scottsdale High School - 7410 E. Indian School Road
Scottsdale Community College - 9000 E. Chaparral Road

Tennis

Comanche Park - 7639 Via de los Ninos
(other facilities charge fees)

Volleyball Courts

McCormick Railroad Park - Indian Bend & Scottsdale Road

Tempe

Softball/baseball

Lighted fields
Clark Park - 19th Street & Roosevelt
Papago Park - North Mill & Curry Road
Unlit fields
Daley Park - Encanto Drive & College Avenue
Kiwanis Community Park - Baseline Road & Western Canal
Tempe Beach Park - First Street & Mill Avenue

Racquetball

All high schools in Tempe have outdoor handball courts that are useable as racquetball courts. However, two high schools have lighted courts:

McClintock High School - 1830 E. Del Rio
Marcos De Niza High School - 6000 S. Lakeshore Drive

Shuffleboard

Clark Park - 19th Street & Roosevelt

Special Sporting Activity

Tubing on the Salt River

Tubing down the Salt River is one of the most enjoyable FREE attractions in Arizona. Located on the Salt River in the Tonto National Forest, one of the best places to begin your voyage is the Blue Point Bridge.

To get there, drive east on McKelleps Road to Bush Highway. At Bush Highway, turn left. Continue on about 10 miles to Blue Point Bridge over the Salt River. If you don't want to take two cars (one for the starting point, and one for the finish line), you can use a shuttle bus service for a fee. Contact Salt River Recreational Incorporated at Bush Highway and Usery Pass, telephone 984-3305. In summer the Salt River can be chilly. Also, it is easy to get a severe sunburn; so take precautions.

CHAPTER 14

MORE FREE THINGS

Bayless Cracker Barrel Store

This quasi-museum re-creates a well-stocked general store, circa 1890. Many old fashioned food and candy displays can be seen, as well as numerous interesting historical exhibits. Open Tuesday through Saturday 10 a.m. to 6 p.m.; Sunday 11 a.m. to 5 p.m.; closed Mondays and holidays. Located at 118 W. Indian School Road, in Phoenix.

Boothill Graveyard

Tombstone, Arizona (located North of the city limits.) This now famous spot contains the graves of some 180 outlaws and unsavory characters. Donations, but no entrance fee.

Books on Wildlife, Birds, Desert Survival

Some of the best writing on the subject and it's yours free of charge. For a current list of titles still in print, write:
Arizona Game & Fish Dept.
2222 W. Greenway Road
Phoenix, Arizona 85023

A few available booklets;

Bird-Watchers Checklist Amateur

A list of nearly 500 birds known to occur in Arizona—all set to be marked by the amateur bird-watcher who likes to keep a record of the species he has seen.

Birder's Checklist of Arizona's Birds

A checklist of some 500 birds known to occur in Arizona -arranged in the phylogenetic order familiar to experienced ornithologists and birders.

Do You Value Your Privilege To Hunt And Fish?

A small handout describing the two main reasons Arizonans are losing their privilege to hunt and fish.

Hunting And Fishing In Arizona

A pamphlet designed to provide basic information, as indicated by the title.

Sportsman's Pocket Fact Sheet

A small pocket fact sheet that contains pertinent facts that can be used to answer those people who condemn hunting and claim hunters are destroying our wildlife.

Camping Grounds For City Folk

El Dorado Urban Campground. Palm Lane and 76th Street in Scottsdale. Telephone 994-2483 The first of its kind in the U.S., the El Dorado Urban Campground is a pilot project by the City of Scottsdale and the federal government to provide urban residents of Scottsdale, Phoenix and other Valley communities with a place to experience camping out *right in the city!*

The campground includes sites for 30 families or groups, along with ramadas, picnic facilities and a small fishing lake. The pioneer recreational facility *(not open to travelers!)* is administered by the Scottsdale Parks & Recreational Department, which maintains emergency facilities at the site, and a staff of campground supervisors.

Stays are limited to one night in order to give as many people as possible an opportunity to take advantage of the campground—*and reservations are a must!* As can be easily imagined, the facility goes over great with city-raised youngsters.

Camelback Mountain

Located between Phoenix and Scottsdale on Camelback Road, the famous Valley landmark is so-named because its profile from a distance resembles that of a giant camel. Many enjoy hiking and climbing the mountain. Despite its relative modest size, some of the slopes are quite steep and extremely dangerous for the novice climber.

Fountain Hills

About 30 minutes northeast of Scottsdale (40 minutes from Phoenix) on the slope of McDowell Mountains, Fountain Hills is a "total community" development of McCulloch Properties, Inc., the same company that created Lake Havasu City. Besides a spectacular location (it is bounded on the north by the McDowell Mountain Regional Park, on the south by the Salt River Indian Reservation and on the east by the Verde River Valley—and offers a magnificent view of the Superstition Mountains), Fountain Hills is growing according to a master plan that covers every aspect of the community from its golf courses and horse-riding trails to the special areas for light industry.

Eventually, Fountain Hills will have a population of 70,000; which will amount to less than six persons per acre, as compared to 40 to 80 persons per acre in most unplanned cities. Landmark of the Community is a fountain that shoots a plume of water 560 feet into the air. To reach, drive east on Shea Boulevard.

Four Corners

Located on US 160 about 35 miles northwest of Shiprock, New Mexico and so-named because four states meet here: Arizona, Colorado, New Mexico and Utah. This is the only place in the U.S. this occurs. Worth a visit just to tell your grandchildren you were here. The juncture is marked by a concrete monument with the seal of each state.

Free Wildlife Newspaper

The Arizona Game & Fish Department publishes a monthly newspaper called *Wildlife Views,* which is distributed free to Arizona residents. To request a free subscription, call or write the Game & Fish Department.

Grady Gammage Auditorium

Designed by the late Frank Lloyd Wright, this imposing structure is at Arizona State University in Tempe. It is a center for numerous cultural events throughout the year, and itself is a popular visitor's attraction. To see, drive to Tempe (via Van Buren or Washington from Phoenix) on the main East-West highway.

Green Valley

A beautiful retirement community 20 miles south of Tucson on Highway 89 (toward Nogales), *Green Valley*dates from 1964. The architectural theme is Spanish modern, and the community sets on a broad sloping valley that provides a superb view of the Santa Rita Mountains. Resort-type recreational facilities and other amenities make *Green Valley* one of the most desirable retirement communities in the state.

Green Valley currently has a permanent population of approximately 8,000, and is still growing. Up to 2,000 visitors also spend each winter there. Eighty percent of the population, both permanent and visiting, is over the age of 65.

Amenities in Green Valley are oriented toward its senior citizen residents, with the accent on recreational and hobby facilities. The community has a medical clinic, operated by Southern Pacific Hospitals, its own weekly newspaper, fire department and sheriff's substation. There is one elementary and one high school.

Besides its proximity to many interesting attractions (national monuments; Sabino Canyon; Nogales, Mexico; Tucson's Living Desert Museum, etc.), Green Valley gains a great deal from its weather. Some average daytime highs: January 58.4 degrees; April 74.8; July 91.1; October 78.9. Average lows for the same months: January 36.6; April 49.3; July 67.8 and October 55.3. The community gets an average of 19.7 inches of rainfall each year, but enjoys sunshine 85 percent of the time.

Hunt's Tomb

On a hill in Papago Park, in Phoenix, the white pyramid marks the burial place of Arizona's first governor, George W.P. Hunt, who served 7 terms.

Japanese Flower Gardens

From early November to June, another of the *must* drives in the Valley of the Sun is on Baseline Road along the waist of South Mountain. This drive takes you along a 2-mile stretch of flower farms, mostly owned and operated by Americans of Japanese descent, which present one of the most colorful sights to be seen.

The farms grow and ship flowers to all parts of the nation. For the convenience of visitors and residents, they have flower-stands along the drive where passers-by can stop and make up their own bouquets from freshly cut flowers.

The peak blooming period is in February, March and April. From Phoenix, drive south on Central Avenue to Baseline Road and turn east. From Scottsdale, drive south on Scottsdale Road to Baseline Road and turn west.

Lake Powell (near Page, AZ)

This 180 mile long lake is one of the finest you will ever see. It is one of the best for camping, swimming, boating and fishing. There are free tours of The Glen Canyon Dam which created Lake Powell. The total shoreline is over 1,900 miles.

The Lavender Pit (Bisbee)

Over a million tons of concentrated ore was mined here when it was an open pit copper mine. The ore was worth about $25 million. The pit can be viewed from US 80, which skirts a bench of the pit.

Lowell Observatory (Flagstaff)

This is one of the foremost astronomical observatories in the country. The planet Pluto was discovered here in 1930. Tickets should be obtained from Chamber of Commerce for free lecture and slide show during the summer. The Chamber is at 101 W. Santa Fe.

The observatory is on Mars Hill, 1 mile west via Santa Fe Avenue.

Libraries

Phoenix's main city library, in a beautiful building of contemporary Southwestern design, is at Central and McDowell. It is open Monday thru Thursday from 10 a.m. to 9 p.m. and on Friday and Saturday from 10 a.m. to 6 p.m. Sunday hours are from 2 p.m. to 6 p.m. Closed on Sundays during June, July and August. Telephone 262-6451

The Scottsdale Public Library is in the Scottsdale Civic Center, at 3839 Civic Center Plaza. Telephone 994-2471. Hours are 10 a.m. to 9 p.m. Monday thru Thursday; 10 a.m. to 5 p.m. Friday and Saturday; and 1 to 5 p.m. on Sunday from September thru May. Branches are located at 7700 E. Roosevelt (994-2329) and 7305 N. Indian Bend (994-2374).

Glendale Public Library, 710 N. 58th Avenue. (931-5576).

Tempe Public Library, 3500 S. Rural Road. (968-8231).

Mesa Public Library, 59 E. 1st Street. (834-2207).

McCormick Ranch

McCormick Ranch located in Scottsdale is a magnificent 3,000 acre community of resorts, recreational facilities, homes and town houses. It is so named because the famous owner of the *Chicago Tribune,* John McCormick actually owned a ranch on the property.

A good place to begin your drive around McCormick Ranch is Scottsdale Road and McCormick Parkway. You will note colorful Camelback Lake with its sailboats, ducks and shoreline.

There are two resorts along the way: McCormick Inn and The Scottsdale Conference Center. Both are worth a stroll around the grounds. In summary, this is a "must see" attraction.

Mesa's Mormon Temple

The impressive architecture and beautifully landscaped grounds of the Temple of the Church of Jesus Christ of Latter-Day Saints makes this one of the most photographed attractions in the state. Free guide service is available daily from 9 a.m. to 9 p.m. from the Temple Information Office, 101 S. Lesueur, Mesa.

Mesa — University of Arizona Experiment Station

Located at 1601 W. Main Street, it is of interest to experts and specialists. The station's primary function is in the area of insect control and research regarding vegetables. Tours can be arranged by appointment. Phone 964-1725.

Montezuma's Well

This is a limestone sinkwell about 11 miles northeast of the famous Montezuma's Castle (entrance fee.) Rimmed by pueblos and cliff dwellings, it is 470 feet wide and 55 feet deep. It is located at a clearly marked exit on I-17 North near Camp Verde. Daily 7 a.m. to 7 p.m. in summer; 8 a.m. to 5 p.m. the rest of the year.

The Amazing Quartzsite Pow Wow

The little sleepy desert town of Quartzsite, Arizona population 1,200, swells to 750,000 beginning the first Thursday in February.

Thousands of dealers offer handcrafted wares; while others sell or trade rocks, gems and jewelry throughout the weekend. This event has now attained international attention. The town is off I-10 near the Arizona-California border, east of Blythe, California.

Rawhide

An Arizona Western town circa 1880, Rawhide takes the visitor back to Territorial days. Complex has everything one would expect to find in a town of that era, including a blacksmith shop, jail, a corral with a wagon display, etc. Special features include exhibits of glass-blowing, a gun display, Indian jewelry, Western wear and more. A General Store has sandwiches, a soda fountain and a candy-making machine. Authentic mementos on display include Geronimo's moccasins, Tom Mix's hat and boots, and Belle Starr's furniture. The Golden Belle Restaurant serves cowboy steaks and barbecue chicken, and has Western music and dancing.

To reach, drive north on Scottsdale Road to just before Pinnacle Peak Rd. There is no admission charge and parking is free. Hours are 5 p.m. to midnight on weekdays; noon to midnight on weekends. Tel. 992-6111.

St. John's Indian Mission

A mission school run by Franciscan Fathers at Komatke on the Pima Indian Reservation, St. John's is about 17 miles southwest of Phoenix. Visitors are welcome, but must obtain permission to go through the grounds from the Father in charge. Tel. 243-4303.

To reach the mission, drive west on Van Buren to 51st Avenue, turn left and follow the signs. A public picnic-bazaar is held annually at the school about the first Sunday in March. Visitors flock there to enjoy the midway rides, buy Indian handicrafts and dine on Indian-style barbecued beef.

Scottsdale Center for the Arts

Designed by famed Arizona architect Bennie Gonzales, the *Scottsdale Center for the Arts,* at 3839 Civic Center Plaza, includes a main theater that will seat up to 822; a 175-seat cinema; an arts exhibition gallery; a multi-use rehearsal hall; conference rooms; and a carpeted atrium-lobby that encompasses nearly one-quarter of an acre.

The basic theme of the Scottsdale Center for the Arts is that it is by and for the people. The facilities are meant to be used by interested groups. City exhibits in the gallery are changed regularly. Besides stage presentations, the theaters show outstanding American and foreign films of the last 20 years — most of which have never appeared in local commercial theaters. For events and ticket information, call the Center Box Office at 994-2381.

Sun City and Sun City West

Seventeen miles west of Phoenix on Grand Avenue (Highways 70-80-89), Del Webb's planned retirement communities are world-famous, and a major attraction for Americans as well as visitors from abroad.

In addition to all the facilities and services of a metropolitan city, Sun City has a wide range of recreational and entertainment facilities designed especially for retired senior citizens. One of the most spectacular of these is a large man-made boating and fishing lake.

Tucson Community Center

The *Tucson Community Center,*at Main and Congress downtown, is the cultural heart of the city. Completed in early 1971 (and the first entertainment and convention center of its kind in Arizona), the complex includes an auditorium and music hall for ice shows, variety shows, sporting events, circuses and mass meeting; plus a "History Area" depicting scenes from the city's colorful past. Box Office telephone 791-4266.

SHOPPING AS A PASTIME IN THE VALLEY OF THE SUN

Phoenix, Scottsdale and adjoining communities are a shopper's mecca, not only from the viewpoint of the number of shops and stores and the variety of merchandise available, but also because of the convenience and beauty of so many of the facilities. Some of the shopping streets and malls are in fact, tourist attractions.

While there are hundreds of specialty and service shops, clustered along several main thoroughfares and streets, shopping malls and shopping centers are responsible for the special character of shopping in the Valley of the Sun. They include:

Shopping Centers in Phoenix

Biltmore Fashion Park Shopping Center: 24th St. & Camelback Road. Designed for beauty, comfort and convenience, this showplace includes The Broadway Department Store and branches of Sak's 5th Avenue, I. Magnin's, Elizabeth Arden's, and Doubleday Book Shops. Regular hours are 10 a.m. to 5:30 p.m., with some shops open until 9 p.m. on Thursdays.

Chris-Town Mall: 15th Avenue & Bethany Home Road. One of the largest enclosed and air-conditioned shopping malls in the country (with over 100 shops and stores), Chris-Town functions as a home-away-from-home. Its major tenants arc Penney's, The Broadway, Bullocks, Montgomery Ward, Abbotts, Hanny's, Switzer's, Farrels Ice Cream Parlor, six theaters, several restaurants, Hunter's Books, and more. Most of the shops open at 10 a.m. Most are open until 9 p.m.

Park Central Shopping Center: 3300 N. Central Avenue. Midway between downtown and the north end of the popular "Central Corridor," Park Central is another onestop center, with over 50 stores. Among them: Goldwater's, Diamond's, Penney's, Switzer's, Hanny's, several restaurants including Fat Frank's (with patio tables), a Community Box Office (2nd fl. of Diamond's), an automotive center, a key shop, Singer Sewing Ccnter, B. Dalton Book Shop, etc. Most of the stores open at 10 a.m.

Thomas Mall Shopping Center: 45th Street & E. Thomas Road. Another enclosed shopping mecca with over 90 stores, including Diamond's, Montgomery Ward, Switzer's, Cheese House & Wine Barrel, Maharani Creations, Chin's Imports, The Gap (lots of teenage stuff), B. Dalton Book Shop, Fry's Grocery, KBUZ Radio Station, and more. Hours here are from 10 a.m. with late nights on Mondays, Thursdays and Fridays.

Town & Country Shopping Center: 21st Street & E. Camelback Road. Biggest claim to fame here is *The Food Bazaar* which features 7 different kinds of food, from Chinese to German. Also has many stores and shops, including Smitty's Big Town, Tang's Imports, Alpine Ski Keller, Starrett's, plus four other restaurants serving Mexican, Polynesian, American and seafood respectively. Shops are open 10 a.m. to 6 p.m. on regular days and to 9 p.m. on Thursdays.

Tower Plaza Shopping Center: 3715 E. Thomas Road. There are over 50 shops in this center but it is best known for the *Ice Palace* skating rink and its Cinema Theater. Stores include Penney's. From 9:30 and 10 a.m.

Uptown Plaza Shopping Center: Camelback Road & Central Avenue. Completely refurbished in 1973, this popular North Central complex has numerous shops (Arizona Town & Country, LuAnn's, Cheese House) and the well-known Navarre's Restaurant. From 9 and 10 a.m.

MetroCenter: Peoria Avenue & Black Canyon Highway. This spectacular two-level shopping center is one of the largest such complexes in the state, with nearly 200 stores. Among them: Sears, The Broadway, Joske's, Diamond's and Goldwater's. Elaborately designed and landscaped, and already a "tourist" attraction.

Westridge Mall: Another of the fabulous weather-controlled shopping malls in the Valley of the Sun, Westridge is at 7611 W. Thomas Road, and serves the western side of the Valley. Major stores include Sears and Penney's, and there are boutiques and specialty shops galore. Hours are 10 a.m. to 9 p.m. Monday thru Friday; 10 a.m. to 6 p.m. on Saturday and noon to 5 p.m. on Sunday.

In Scottsdale

Scottsdale Fashion Square: Camelback & Scottsdale Roads. Fashion Square was Scottsdale's first major shopping center. Has a Goldwater's Dept. Store, Diamond's, a Bayless Market, Doubletree Inn, popular restaurants and book shops. Most stores on the premises open at 10 a.m. Very attractive setting.

Los Arcos Mall: McDowell & Scottsdale Rds. One of the most beautiful shopping centers in the Southwest, Los Arcos (The Arches) has numerous stores and specialty shops. (The Broadway, Sears, Starrett's, Gold Art, Godber's Indian Jewelry & Gifts, Robinson's Accents, Walden Book Shop) in air-conditioned comfort, making shopping there an experience. Most shops open at 10 a.m. on weekdays; at noon on Sundays.

Fifth Avenue: A landmark as well as a sightseeing attraction, Scottsdale's *Fifth Avenue* is one of Arizona's most unusual and interesting shopping streets. It consists of dozens of specialty shops, both posh and picturesque, offering a wide variety of high-fashion women's wear, accessories, gifts, art products, crafts and books.

Paradise Valley Mall: Serving Paradise Valley and the northeast environs of Phoenix, this beautiful mall has the usual array of boutiques and speciality shops, along with a Penney's, Diamond's and Goldwater's. There are also restaurants, theaters and a game room. One of the most popular free attractions of the mall is that it is a "joggers' paradise." Monday thru Saturday the mall is open from 6:15 a.m. to 9:30 a.m. and on Sundays from 7 a.m. to 11 a.m. *for joggers!* Regular hours are 10 a.m. to 9 p.m. Monday thru Friday; 10 a.m. to 6 p.m. on Saturday and noon to 5 p.m. on Sunday. The mall is located on the northwest corner of Cactus Road and Tatum Blvd.

Main Street: Both sides of Main Street, east and west of Scottsdale Road are also lined with picturesque specialty shops and restaurants, and is another of the city's major attractions.

CamelView Plaza: 6900 E. Camelback Road. Another of Scottsdale's showplace shopping centers, CamelView Plaza stores and shops include Sakowitz, Bullock's, Lillie Rubin (from Miami), Margo's La Mode (from Dallas), and a Walden Book Store—plus twin CamelView Cinema theaters. Two-level underground parking as well as surface parking.

In Mesa

Fiesta Mall: Junction of Alma School Road and Southern Avenue. Modern-looking and popular with over 100 shops including major department stores: Sears, Diamond's, Broadway, several good restaurants. Ample parking space, stroller rentals (fee), and other convenient features. One of the newer malls in the Valley.

Tri-City Mall: 1900 W. Main. More or less midway between Mesa, Tempe and Scottsdale, the Tri-City Mall shopping center serves all three communitites. Its shops and stores include Penney's, Diamond's, Hanny's, Switzer's, National Shirt, etc., plus a Sun Garden Cafeteria and other eating places. Hours are from 10 a.m. on weekdays; from noon on Sundays.

In Cave Creek

Frontier Town: As picturesque as its name implies, Cave Creek's *Frontier Town* shopping center has some two dozen stores, including the Frontier Trading Post, Arts & Flowers, the World of Glass, Scorpion Boutique, The Washboard, G-S Leather Shop, Corral of Sweets, and the Silver Spur Restaurant & Saloon (a family-type place with live entertainment nightly). If you find Cave Creek (on Cave Creek Road, NE of Phoenix; N of Scottsdale), you can't miss Frontier Town. It's the town's downtown.

In Carefree

Spanish Village: The accent here is elegant Spanish and the result is one of the most picturesque and attractive specialty shopping centers in Arizona. Among its shops are Vivian's, Dos Podros, Sculpture West, Black Mountain Leather, Carefree Goldsmith, Grey Metate (Navajo Indian Jewelry), and a popular El Toro Restaurant & Cantina. Has a beautiful inner courtyard and an open-air patio for dining.

SHOPPING IN TUCSON

Shopping facilities in Tucson can be divided into three categories: specialty shops, markets and department or variety stores, and shopping centers.

The city's specialty shops, ranging from Indian trading posts and art galleries to high fashion boutiques, are clustered along several main thoroughfares, including E. Broadway, Stone in the downtown area, E. Speedway, Campbell and Oracle Road—often in conjunction with neighborhood markets and department stores.

In the shopping center category, Tucson has several elaborate centers and over two dozen so-called "Strip" shopping centers—which means they take up one, two, or three blocks along a street, at an intersection or in a plaza, and incorporate from half a dozen to two or three dozen stores and shops.

Shopping Centers

El Con Shopping Center: 3601 E. Broadway. Tel. 326-1051. The largest shopping center in Southern Arizona, El Con has a completely air-conditioned mall, and parking for over 7,000 cars. Major stores at El Con are Ward's, Penney's, Steinfield's, Levy's, Goldwater's, Lerner's, Dave Bloom & Sons, Hallmark Cards, the Walden Book Store and El Con Book Store. City buses Nos. 3, 8 and 11 serve the El Con Shopping Center daily.

Park Mall Shopping Center: Completely enclosed, with over 80 stores (including Broadway, Diamond's, and Sears), the huge Park Mall also has theaters and several restaurants on the premises. Located at Broadway and Wilmot.

Downtown: The downtown section of Tucson, along Stone Avenue and the adjoining streets, is also a major shopping area. Its landmark stores include Jacome's, Penney's, Myerson's, Lerner's and various specialty shops and restaurants.

La Placita Village: 102 W. Broadway. "Little Mexico" in downtown Tucson. Still new, dozens of shops, plus craftsmen at work. Other attractions include restaurants, discotheques and an art gallery.

"Strip" Shopping Centers

Best known and largest of the so-called "Strip" shopping centers—many of which are very attractive, from both a posh and picturesque viewpoint—include the following:

Campbell Plaza, 2800 N. Campbell.
Casas Adobes, Ina Road at the Florence Highway.
Amphi Plaza, North 1st Avenue & Fort Lowell Road.
Southgate Shopping Center, 3370 S. 6th Avenue.
Pavilion Shopping Plaza, 4656 N. Oracle Road.
Broadway Village, Broadway & Country Club Road.
County Fair, 22nd St. & Craycroft.
Broadway 7000, Broadway & Kolb.
Monterey Village, Speedway & Wilmot.
Oxford Plaza, 22nd St. & Wilmot.

Trail Dust Town

This is a shopping-dining center done up in the style of the Old West, at 6541 Tanque Verde Road. Besides numerous unusual shops, there is a Trading Post, an art gallery, an Ice Cream Palace and two noted steak houses: Pinnacle Peak and Sneeky Pete's.

CHAPTER 15

ARIZONA ROAD & WEATHER TIPS

Before setting out on an auto trip in Arizona, especially in summer, check your battery, air conditioning, hose connections and tire pressure. Some drivers carry an extra set of hoses in the car as well as a gallon of distilled water for any emergency. Be certain that your spare tire is usuable and that the car is properly tuned up to ensure better gas mileage.

SPECIAL WARNING

Desert Travel

Don't leave the established highways and roads in Arizona for a tour of the desert without an experienced guide and careful preparation. Desert temperatures can soar and fatally dehydrate a person in four to six hours. It is easy to become disoriented and lost in the desert when only minutes from well-traveled highways.

Dust Storms

Severe dust storms in Arizona can strike with savage fury, making driving conditions hazardous on many stretches of highway. The areas hardest hit by dust storms in the state include Interstate 10 between Phoenix and Tucson and I-8 from Gila Bend to Casa Grande.

A system of dust warning signs are posted on I-10 and I-8 to advise motorists of conditions. In such a storm, blinding, choking dust drops visibility to zero, causing accidents that can involve a chain of vehicles. The dust storms rapidy transform normal driving into a nightmare for passengers and driver.

What To Do In A Dust Storm

1. Remain calm.
2. If dense dust is observed blowing across the roadway, do **NOT** enter the area.
3. Pull vehicle off the pavement as far as possible, stop, turn your lights OFF, set the emergency brake.
4. If conditions prevent pulling off the roadway, proceed at a reduced speed, turn lights ON and use the center lane as a guide.

Dust storm alerts are broadcast on three local Phoenix stations: KOY 560, KTAR 620 and KJJJ 910. In Tucson, you can get dust storm information on KTUC 1300.

Flash Floods

When violent thunderstorms break over the mountains and deserts of the Southwest, runoff from the torrential rain cascades into canyons, gullies and washes in a matter of minutes. Walls of water, sometimes 10 to 30 feet high, swirl downward picking up trees, mud and debris. Tragically, plants, animals and in some cases, people are caught, swept along and battered by the onrushing torrent. It is possible to be picnicking in a low lying area where the sun is actually shining and be victims of this kind of flash flood. The flash flood can result from a severe thunderstorm centered over mountains many miles away.

Most flash floods in Arizona, occur in summer and early fall. The Army Corps of Engineers and National Weather Service have prepared a checklist for survival in flash floods:

1. Always carry survival gear. In hot weather in desert areas, allow 3-4 gallons of water per day per person.
2. Listen frequently to radio weather reports.
3. Establish campsites on **high ground,** but not on top of exposed peaks or ridges.
4. Avoid deep canyons and dry washes during stormy or threatening weather.
5. If a thunderstorm strikes, **move to high ground immediately.** If you cannot move your vehicle out of a low-lying area, **leave.** Many lives have been lost needlessly because people fail to heed the warnings of park rangers, police officers and other officials.
6. Inform someone of your destination and when you expect to return from your trip. Police should be notified **immediately** if you fail to return on time.
7. Keep an eye on the sky for thunderstorm activity.

Too Hot To Handle

Carry a small towel to place over your steering wheel when parking outside in the summer. Most important: don't leave children or pets in your vehicle unattended during summer months.

Gasoline

Be sure you have plenty of gasoline in the car before setting out on a trip. Arizona is a big state and there is often long stretches of highway to go before you come to a service station. If you run out of gas in a sparsely populated area, few passerbys will be able to help.

Water

Always carry an ample supply of drinking water, especially before entering any remote area.

Breakdowns

If you breakdown on a road in Arizona, raise the hood of your car to alert the Highway Patrol. In remote areas, stay with your car and out of the sun in summer. However, if you must go for help, wait until after dark. Convince the others in the car to stay there. Return along the same route you took to seek help.

Winter Driving

Arizona *does* have a winter, especially in the northern section of the state. If your trip to this area is in winter, listen to advance weather reports. There are times when chains and snow tires are needed.

CHAPTER 16

OTHER INFORMATION SOURCES

ARIZONA CHAMBERS OF COMMERCE

Alpine Chamber of Commerce
P.O. Box 410
Alpine, AZ 85920
(602) 339-4588

Apache Junction Chamber of Commerce
P.O. Box 101
Apache Junction, AZ 85220
(602) 982-3141

Avondale-Goodyear
Litchfield Park
Chamber of Commerce
P.O. Box 327
Avondale, AZ 85323
(602) 932-2260

Benson Chamber of Commerce
P.O. Box AQ
Benson, AZ 85602
(602) 586-2842

Bisbee Chamber of Commerce
P.O. Drawer BA
Bisbee, AZ 85603
(602) 432-2141

Buckeye Chamber of Commerce
P.O. Box 717
Buckeye AZ 85326
(602) 386-2727

Bullhhead City
P.O. Box 66
Bullhead City, AZ 86430
(602) 754-3891

Carefree Chamber of Commerce
P.O. Box 734
Carefree, AZ 85377
(602) 488-3381

Casa Grande Chamber of Commerce
316 East Fourth Street
Casa Grande, Az 85222
(602) 836-2125

Coolidge Chamber of Commerce
320 West Central Avenue
Coolidge, AZ 85228
(602) 723-3009

Parker Area Chamber of Commerce
P.O. Box 627
Parker, AZ 85344
(602) 669-2174

Payson Chamber of Commerce
Drawer A
Payson, AZ 85541
(602) 474-4515

Phoenix, & Valley of The Sun Convention & Visitors Bureau
2701 E. Camelback Road, Suite 200 H.
Phoenix, AZ 85016
(602) 957-0070

Pima Chamber of Commerce
P.O. Box 363
Pima, AZ 85543
(602) 428-2486

Pine-Strawberry Chamber of Commerce
P.O. Box 196
Pine, AZ 85544

Prescott Chamber of Commerce
P.O. Box 1147
Prescott, AZ 86302
(602) 445-2000

Safford-Graham County Chamber of Commerce
1111 Thatcher Boulevard
Safford, AZ 85546
(602) 428-2511

St. Johns Chamber of Commerce
P.O. Box 577
St. Johns, AZ 85936
(602) 337-4766

Scottsdale Chamber of Commerce
P.O. Box 129
Scottsdale, AZ 85252
(602) 945-8481

Sedona-Oak Creek Canyon Chamber of Commerce
P.O. Box 478
Sedona AZ 86336
(602) 282-7722

Show Low Chamber of Commerce
P.O. Box 1083
Show Low, AZ 85901
(602) 537-2326

Sierra Vista Chamber of Commerce
372 North Garden Avenue
Sierra Vista, AZ 85635
(602) 458-6940

Tempe Chamber of Commerce
504 East Southern Avenue
Tempe, AZ 85282
(602) 967-7891

Tolleson Chamber of Commerce
P.O. Box 625
Tolleson, AZ 85353
(602) 936-3363

Tombstone Chamber of Commerce
Box 67
Tombstone, AZ 85638
(602) 457-3552

Tucson Metropolitan Chamber of Commerce
P.O. Box 991
Tucson, AZ 85702
(602) 792-2250

Douglas Chamber of
Commerce
P.O. Box Drawer F
Douglas, AZ 85607
(602) 364-2477

Flagstaff Chamber of
Commerce
101 West Santa Fe
Flagstaff, AZ 86001
(602) 774-4505

Fountain Hills Chamber of
Commerce
P.O. Box 17598
Fountain Hills AZ 85268
(602) 837-1654

Gila Bend Chamber of
Commerce
P.O. Box CC
Gila Bend AZ 85337
(602) 683-2261

Gilbert Chamber of
Commerce
P.O. Box 527
Gilbert AZ 85234
(602) 892-0056

Glendale District Chamber
of Commerce
7125 North 58th Drive
Glendale, AZ 85301
(602) 937-4754

Globe Chamber of
Commerce
P.O. Box 2539
Globe, AZ 85501
(602) 425-4495

Greenlee County Chamber of
Commerce
P.O. Box 1237
Clifton, AZ 85533
(602) 865-3313

Greer Chamber of Commerce
P.O. Box 254
Greer AZ 85297
(602) 735-7583

Kearny Chamber of
Commerce
P.O. Box 206
Kearny, AZ 85237
(602) 363-5554

Kingman Area Chamber of
Commerce
P.O. Box 1150
Kingman, AZ 86402
(602) 753-6106

Lake Havasu Area Chamber
of Commerce
2074 McCulloch Boulevard
Lake Havasu City, AZ 86403
(602) 855-4115

Mesa Chamber of Commerce
10 West 1st Street
Mesa, AZ 85201
(602) 969-1307

Miami Chamber of
Commerce
511 Live Oak Street
Miami, AZ 85539
(602) 473-3871

Nogales-Santa Cruz County
Chamber of Commerce
Kino Park
Nogales, AZ 85621
(602) 287-3685

Oatman Chamber of
Commerce
P.O. Box 423
Oatman, AZ 86433

Page-Lake Powell Chamber
of Commerce
P.O. Box 727
Page, AZ 86040
(602) 645-2741

Tucson Convention &
Visitors Bureau
P.O. Box 27210
Tucson, AZ 85726
(602) 791-4768

Verde Valley Chamber of
Commerce
P.O. Box 412
Cottonwood, AZ 86326
(602) 634-2912

White Mountain Chamber of
Commerce
P.O. Box 181
Springerville, AZ 85938
(602) 333-2123

Wickenburg Chamber of
Commerce
P.O. Drawer CC
Wickenburg, AZ 85358
(602) 684-5479

Willcox Chamber of
Commerce
754 South Haskell Avenue
Willcox, AZ 85643
(602) 384-2272

Williams-Grand Canyon
Chamber of Commerce
P.O. Box 235
Williams, AZ 86046
(602) 635-2041

Yarnell-Peeples Valley
Chamber of Commerce
P.O. Box 275
Yarnell, AZ 85362
(602) 427-6374

Yuma County Chamber of
Commerce
P.O. Box 230
Yuma, AZ 85364
(602) 782-2567

Road & Weather Information
(602) 262-8261

Leisure Listings

The Arizona Republic, published in Phoenix for state-wide distribution, carries a regular Friday feature page called *Bookin' it* in its Leisure Section. The page is a calendar of forthcoming attractions, lectures, exhibits, concerts, bicycle rides, foot races, hikes, classes, festivals and other activities, many of which are free. On most occasions, the listings include several that are for children.

In the summer months, *Bookin' it* includes information about camping around the state.

OTHER SOURCES OF INFORMATION

Arizona Game & Fish Department
2222 West Greenway Road
Phoenix, AZ 86607

Arizona State Parks Board
1688 West Adams
Phoenix, AZ 85007

Arizona Outdoor Recreation
Coordinating Commission
4433 North 19th Avenue
Phoenix, AZ 85015

The Bureau of Land Management (BLM)
Phoenix, District Office
201 North Central Avenue
Phoenix, Az 85003

(Consult the phone book in other areas for additional district offices, such as in Safford, Yuma and other cities.)

National Park Service
Southern Arizona Group
1115 N 1st Street
Phoenix, AZ 85004

Arizona State Office of Tourism
3507 N. Central Avenue
Phoenix, AZ 85012

(Ask for the Arizona Road Map. It is published and distributed FREE by ARIZONA HIGHWAYS MAGAZINE.)